Writing Strategies for Talent Development

Writing Strategies for Talent Development helps educators incorporate effective and engaging writing strategies into their classrooms that are designed to reach struggling and gifted students alike. This guide demonstrates how teachers can provide the means to write (with appropriate tools and classroom structures), the motivation to write (through engaging genre-based lessons), and the opportunity to write more frequently across multiple subjects. Covering genres from fantasy, crime, and humor, to horror, non-fiction, and even romance, this book provides the tools to support every writer in the room.

Jennifer Gottschalk writes, talks about writing, and thinks about writing every day. Over the past 20 years in education, Jennifer has worked with students in Grades 2–12. During the school year she can be found co-planning, co-teaching, or demo teaching writing lessons in classrooms across the Denver metro area.

Other Eye On Education Books Available From Routledge
(www.routledge.com/k-12)

Creating Inclusive Writing Environments in the K-12 Classroom: Reluctance,
Resistance, and Strategies that Make a Difference
Angela Stockman

The Middle School Grammar Toolkit: Using Mentor Texts to Teach Standards-
Based Language and Grammar in Grades 6–8, Second Edition
Sean Ruday

Sexuality for All Abilities: Teaching and Discussing
Sexual Health in Special Education
Katie Thune and Molly Gage

Coding as a Playground: Programming and Computational Thinking in the Early
Childhood Classroom, Second Edition
Marina Umaschi Bers

Implementing Project Based Learning in Early Childhood: Overcoming
Misconceptions and Reaching Success
Sara Lev, Amanda Clark, and Erin Starkey

Grit, Resilience, and Motivation in Early Childhood:
Practical Takeaways for Teachers
Lisa B. Fiore

Writing Strategies for Talent Development

From Struggling to Gifted Learners,
Grades 3–8

Jennifer Gottschalk

Routledge
Taylor & Francis Group

NEW YORK AND LONDON

First published 2021
by Routledge
52 Vanderbilt Avenue, New York, NY 10017

and by Routledge
2 Park Square, Milton Park, Abingdon, Oxon, OX14 4RN

Routledge is an imprint of the Taylor & Francis Group, an informa business

Library of Congress Cataloging-in-Publication Data
A catalog record for this title has been requested

ISBN: 9780367544225 (hbk)
ISBN: 9780367543495 (pbk)
ISBN: 9781003089247 (ebk)

Typeset in Optima
by KnowledgeWorks Global Ltd.

Access the Support Material: www.routledge.com/9780367543495

Contents

Preface

Writing Strategies for Talent Development is a book for teachers who know the writers in their classrooms have hidden gifts. Providing the means to write with appropriate tools and classroom structures, the motivation to write through high-interest genre-based lessons, and the opportunity to write more frequently across multiple subjects will yield astonishing results from reluctant writers, do-as-much-as-asked-but-nothing-more writers, and advanced writers.

I once had the opportunity to see Ron Clark speak. [Ron Clark is a famous teacher from the late 90's who had a movie made about him and was on Oprah.] One of the most compelling things he said was along the lines of, "At our school we believe one of our students will be president of the United States someday. But we don't know which one, so we need to prepare them all to be president, just in case." Wouldn't it be cool if we taught writing like this? If we said, "We're confident some students from our school will have writing careers like Lisa Yee or Dav Pilkey but we're not sure which ones, so we want to teach all students all different types of writing, just in case."

I haven't encountered a school using this approach to writing...yet. Most of the time, I work with a grade level or a single classroom and then when the teachers are sharing how happy and excited their students are about writing, that's when these ideas start to spread. The challenge question is "but you're talking about kids who are compliant and who would write because you told them to." And the response is, "No, the kid who threw a desk the last time we asked him to write was also writing. And the one who usually cries and won't do anything? Wrote for thirty minutes today."

It's tricky business to be demo teaching in someone else's classroom. The risk of the receiving teacher linking student engagement and success with the guest teacher rather than with the material is high. To balance this, I've run several "remote support" projects, where I met with the teacher and went through each lesson but didn't meet the students or work with them directly. To my relief and joy, those classes were just as successful as measured by a significant increase in student enthusiasm for writing, engagement with writing, and writing produced.

That's how I know this book will work for you. My favorite teaching books are like having a coach on demand, someone who gives helpful tips and ideas all the way through lessons, especially the lessons I know are going to push my practice. In the spirit of "write what you want to read," I've tried to make this book the kind of writing book I needed when I first started figuring this out for myself and my students.

Acknowledgments

First, thank you to Misha Kydd for seeing the spark of a book idea in my work. Thank you to Olivia Powers for your patience and collaboration on the early drafts. I am incredibly grateful to the team of people at Routledge who helped make this book a reality.

Writing ideas, including the nonfiction ones, start somewhere. Usually with people. Stephanie Meurer, thank you for joining me at the beginning of this journey and co-creating a presentation about gifted writers for the National Association for Gifted Children Conference (NAGC) back in 2005. Thank you also to the facilitators and my fellow teacher-writers in the Colorado Writing Project and the Denver Writing Project, especially Mark Overmeyer, for the inspiration and resources. Thank you to my marvelous students at Cresthill Middle School back in the day, who gave *nearly* every writing idea a try.

Thank you to the incredible writing community in Colorado, especially the fine folks at Rocky Mountain Fiction Writers and Pikes Peak Writers who put on great conferences each year. Watching writers teach each other and learning from professional writers changed me and everything I have done since in my writing classroom. Extra special love to Lisa Brown Roberts and David Slayton – knowing you're both part of the 5 AM writing club and only a text away is a precious gift. James Persichetti, editor extraordinaire, thanks for listening to my teaching ideas and offering hilarious potential titles for this book.

I also owe a tremendous debt of gratitude to the wonderful Gifted community in Colorado. Colleen Anthony, you were the first GT person I told that I wanted to write a book about teaching writing. Like all the best GT teachers, you were supportive and encouraging. It was just a tiny conversation, but I held your warm response close to my nervous writer's heart all these years. Oh and all the words I could write about Dr. Bob Seney. You are the best example of a gifted adult and gifted reader that I have the pleasure to know. Thank you for sharing the treasure of your brilliant mind and the humor that sparkles in your eyes when you talk about books. And of course, thank you to the Colorado Association for Gifted and Talented (CAGT) for so many opportunities to present about writing and gifted writers.

Like writing ideas, teaching ideas come from somewhere, usually students and other teachers.

This book would not have happened without the kindness of Heather Stinnett (and the admin team) at Copper Mesa Elementary who invited me to work with a small group of brilliant, funny 6th graders. That project gave me the confidence to take what I'd made for a creative writing curriculum and turn it into weekly presentations on the ooey-gooey fun of writing genre fiction. A huge, major, sky writing display of thanks to the building leaders and classroom teachers who welcomed me into their schools and classrooms over the last few years.

Like so many teachers, once I had something working, I wanted to expand and change. Thank you, Beth Letzig and Becky Wickstrom at Ranch View Middle School for allowing me to basically live with you and your students over the course of two long projects. To the fourth-grade team at Fox Creek Elementary, thank you for giving me the chance to stretch and grow my skills working with younger students. Thank you to Jessica Simmons and Amber MacFarland for trying all of this on your own as I started considering how the lesson plans might work in another teacher's hands. It was Debbie Clemente who encouraged me to step out of my comfort zone and try presenting these ideas at literacy conferences. And it was Paige Dersham who encouraged me to present my genre fiction thinking for the education strand of Denver Pop Culture Con. Extra special thanks to Debbie, Paige, and my favorite middle school principal, Merry Sillitoe, who read the proposal and some chapters of this book and provided key feedback.

Thank you to the students (and their parents) for granting permission for their work to be shared in this book and with the online resources! Your examples will help writing teachers see more of the possibilities and potential outcomes when writing talent is developed with choice, flexibility, and a sense of humor.

Not everyone is so lucky as me to have acceptance both at work and at home. Thank you to the Douglas County Schools Advanced Academics and Gifted Education team for your unflagging support. Natasha, the best gifted leaders, like the best gifted teachers, find ways to say yes, to encourage passion, and to direct that energy into positive outcomes for all learners. Thank you for saying yes to my writing work.

Finally, heaps and heaps of gratitude to my marvelous extended family, parents, siblings, daughters, and husband. I am a better teacher and better person because of you.

The Means to Write

Writer's Tools

When I was first learning about lesson planning, I often skipped over the "materials" section of teacher books because I didn't think it was important. And then I had a series of teaching challenges because I didn't have enough scissors or sticky notes or tape. When I think about what writers need, the first things I think about now ARE materials: notebook, pencil/pen. Typing onto a device is important too, but devices don't go on sale 4/$1.00 in July. Every summer, I stock up on pens, pencils, and notebooks, just in case. That habit paid off when I worked in a Title 1 middle school because only about 15% of my students came to school with the supplies on the recommended list. I went through my entire stash that year and it was worth it.

Many wonderful books have been written about how to use writer's notebooks in the classroom. I want to add a few procedural things in this section that have worked in my classroom over the years.

1. Notebooks need a home in your classroom, not in desks or backpacks, space permitting. I've kept them on a closet shelf and also in bins. Otherwise, writer's notebooks are easily lost or get used for other things.

2. Treat writer's notebooks with respect and a little bit of ceremony. Create routines for getting them out and putting them away. A writer's notebook routine is a great dividing line between the-subject-we-just-finished in an elementary school classroom and WRITING. Similarly, in middle school, the writer's notebook routine gives students some breathing space and mental transition time while you take attendance and then join them in writing.

3. Notebooks DO NOT go home until the end of the year or the class. This might seem counterintuitive because we *do* want students writing and thinking about writing all the time. The work around, and what I model, is that if I wrote something when I didn't have my writer's notebook, I bring it to school and staple or tape it to the next blank page with the date when I wrote it. I find that I enjoy unfolding and rereading little bits of things I wrote on restaurant receipts, scrap paper, napkins, etc. True story, my fifth novel was based on an idea written on a receipt.

Lesson Ideas

Writer's Tools Day 1 – Decorating and Personalizing Notebooks

On the school supply list, request a notebook that will be just for writing. A regular composition notebook is perfect; a regular single-subject spiral works too. Plan to have plenty of notebooks on hand so that students who didn't bring a notebook can have one of the classroom spares for their own.

For homework the night before, invite students to print and bring in pictures that represent their interests or things that inspire them. Not every student will have access to a printer at home, so have a few fun magazines on hand for cutting out pictures. I also like to put stickers on my computer or my writer's notebook. (Throughout the year, different types of stickers go on sale. Savvy teachers advised me to stock up during all the holidays, not just Valentine's Day.) It's also a good idea to have many colors of permanent marker on hand.

I'm not crafty at all, but I appreciate the intention of decorating my notebook. This designates it as special and different from other notebooks. Sometimes I just go with a really cool notebook design (cool design does not equal expensive or fancy) and don't do much decorating except for stickers. You will have students with this same minimalist approach to notebook decorating. Other students would decorate and collage for the rest of the week. Start your notebook decorating ahead of time but be sure to add a few touches while the students are working. Sometimes my students have really cool ideas and I want to try them too. This is a thing writers do – try other people's ideas. It's not the same as copying, it's like being "inspired by." Good modeling to get out there right at the start.

Depending on the personalities in your classroom, you might need to de-emphasize the artsy aspects of this work and make it about a "custom skin" for the notebook, like really fancy auto detailing or playing with the "design your own" tool on sneaker websites.

Set a time frame for notebook customization; 20–30 minutes is about right. Set a minimum expectation: Student's name First and Last on the inside cover, school year, and for middle school, whichever hour/period the class meets. At least one sticker. Boom. Done.

Dominic Toretto
2021–2022
LA 5th Hour
Mr. Hobbs

Shayna Baszler
2021–2022
4th grade
Ms. Wilde

Some teachers use clear packing tape to seal all the decorating goodness on the notebook covers. This is not necessary but does keep the covers smooth for storage. Some teachers keep each notebook in its own plastic bag and that works just as well, especially if germs are a concern.

As others are finishing decorating, a few will have opened to the first page and started writing or drawing. If so, awesome! If not, no problem. Don't require or prevent any writing right now. Today is about preparing the tools.

When time is up, practice the routine of collecting notebooks. Every teacher has different ways to do this. I asked them to be stacked on the front desk in each row, when we were in rows, and on the table closest to the door, when we were using tables.

Next, if time permits, practice the routine of getting notebooks. In middle school, I put the bin out near the door and students select their notebook as they enter. Or if this is a transition in an elementary classroom, invite four to five students at a time to get their notebooks from the shelf or the bin. If they've put them away and taken them out at least once, the class will be closer to ready for tomorrow.

Why can't the notebooks live in desks, backpacks, lockers, etc.?

- The potential for loss or damage
- Inadvertent use the writers' notebooks for math, social studies, etc.

Pencils or pens? *Whatever works.*

What about tablets/phones/laptops?

- Not yet, except for students who have accommodations for assistive technology. It's nice for students with assistive tech to have notebooks too, in case they want to draw or quick jot ideas on their own or with the help of paraprofessionals.

Writer's Tools – Day 2

Celebrate a successful getting-out-the-notebooks routine. If the routine doesn't work how it should, don't hesitate to put the notebooks away and try again. Teaching routines is a part of classroom management. Throwing notebooks or dropping others' notebooks on the floor is not okay.

Notebooks are ready, everyone has a pen/pencil, and it's time to write. I use the foundations of fiction (character, setting, plot) to introduce writing routines for several reasons. First, students have generally done "small moments" and "memoir" work in earlier grades but they have not written about the things that interest them most, like dragons or people with hidden powers. Second, fiction allows for some emotional distance between the writer and the writing (theoretically) and many students need that emotional distance to brave the blank page.

Make a slide that says the following.

For the next six to eight weeks this is how we will start writing:

- Get your notebooks and something to write with.
- Look at the ideas on the screen.
- Put today's date at the top of the page.
- Write for five minutes without talking to anyone, except possibly the teacher.
- If you don't want to write to what you see that's fine, just write.

The next slide will have the four basic rules for writer's workshop:

1. No co-writing.
2. No characters may be based on anyone in the room/school.
3. Sometimes writing gets personal and we might get overwhelmed by anger or sadness. If this is the case, we will reach out to the mental health team for support.
4. Be mindful of PG (or in some grade levels PG-13) guidelines for kissing, cursing, and killing. Err on the side of school rules if you're not sure, especially for cursing.

For this slide, I usually use a picture of lane lines or train tracks and I explain that my four rules all come from my students and things that went wrong in prior years of writers' workshop.

For Rule 1, ask students to raise their hands if they've ever run a three-legged race. Most have. Then ask, "What's easier, running alone or with a leg tied to someone else?" Co-writing is like running a three-legged race and it's something that experienced professional writers find challenging. Explain that since we're developing writers, we're not going to try that for now.

Although Rule 2 seems self-explanatory, the bottom line is that characters based on people in the room get distracting fast.

For Rule 3, the example I give is that my dog died last Fall, and for a while, my writing got really dark and sad. It was important that I let people know I was having a hard time.

Rule 4 always gets students' attention. And they always understand – they're often happy to have the options of killing, cursing, and kissing even with limitations.

Have students summarize the rules and check for understanding with each other and then it's time to do some writing!

On the next slide, show one interesting picture and one interesting/weird/unusual writing prompt. Explain that sometimes the writing ideas will be words and sometimes pictures.

[Not sure where to look? In an internet search window type "writing prompts" but instead of choosing 'all', choose 'images'. The images can usually be filtered by elementary, middle, and high school as well. Keep folders of these types of things on your desktop. Eventually you'll have enough to organize them by topic.]

Post the following: "Today you will practice the routine of writing silently for five minutes, usually in response to what's on the screen, but of course anything that's okay for school. Use these pictures to get your ideas started." Also add that you will be writing and warming up your thinking while they write. It is not okay for anyone to interrupt you, except for emergencies, for those five minutes.

What's on the screen? Something fun, silly, or startling. This week, especially these first few days, is about changing perception and inviting engagement. The minute you put a goofy cartoon zombie, or an NFL star, or an alligator dressed in a business suit on the screen, your students will begin giving each other the, 'is the principal coming' look or a related concern, 'should someone take the teacher's temperature?'

A scaffold you need to practice here (and probably for at least the first few weeks) is to say: "If you're not sure what to write, copy the words you see on the screen, draw the image, or describe the image in your own words." This scaffold supports everyone engaging in parallel behavior: looking at the screen and moving their pens/pencils in their notebooks. And it starts to erode the habit some students may have which is staring helplessly at the blank page.

Depending on the age of your students and their level of independence, you might need to do a call and response along the lines of:

Teacher: "What will you be doing for the next five minutes?"
Students: "Writing."
Teacher: "What will I be doing for the next five minutes?"
Students: "Writing."
Teacher: "Can you interrupt me?"
Students: "No."
Teacher: "Last thing. Ask the person next to you if they know what to do. Give me a thumbs up when you're confident everyone understands the directions."

Some students will think the call and response are weird, but it is necessary. I can't tell you how many times I was unable to write because students ignored the directions when we didn't practice and double check. And usually, they were asking me, "what are we supposed to do?"

The next routine is the shortest and easiest sharing routine:

After 5 painfully silent minutes have passed, during which you are ignoring everything and also writing to what you see on the screen, call pencils down. Direct the students to look at what they wrote. Ask them to underline their favorite word, phrase, or sentence in their notebook. Then say, "one of the hardest things for writers is to read what they actually wrote instead of telling you about their writing. Turn to a shoulder partner and only read out loud what you underlined."

At this point, hands will go up of students offering to share what they underlined with the whole class. Explain that sharing with the group comes later and we will practice but try not to worry about that now. If you have a student without a partner, share your writing with them.

This is the world's fastest sharing routine and it begins to build community. After all the pairs are finished, ask "did anyone hear something cool or funny or surprising?" A few hands will always go up. Don't ask for sharing out to the group yet though.

Mini-Lesson – Characters

Ask the question, "Are characters the heart of a story? Can you think of any counter examples?" Give students three minutes to jot ideas (no complete sentences required). Facilitate a short class discussion and be sure to note any books mentioned as examples or non-examples of character-centered stories.

Next ask, "What types of characters would make you instantly want to read the book if you saw them on the front or read about them on the back?" Post a few age-specific examples like:

Grades 3–5

- Best friends
- Track stars
- Dragons
- Talking rabbits
- Evil royalty
- Little sisters with special skills

Grades 6–8

- Ghosts with problems
- Evil geniuses
- Cyborgs
- People with hidden powers
- Car thieves
- Scoundrels who help people in secret

Ask students to turn and share their "characters I would read about" lists with a shoulder partner. You should keep a list as well. If time permits, allow them to expand from pairs to fours.

Invite students to add any ideas they heard that they liked to their notebooks. Explain that everyone will be keeping lists of things they like in lots of different categories and that these things might be writing ideas later.

Celebrate a successful completion of the putting-notebooks-away routine.

I adore the "that's what I like" activity and have learned so much about students as a result. One of my favorite moments was as the class was leaving and a small girl with a cherub's face said, "I love it when terrible things happen to small children!" I couldn't help but respond with a grin, "Me too!"

Writer's Tools – Day 3

Celebrate a successful "taking out the notebooks" routine. Notice out loud how much more quickly students are getting settled to write. They may not all be there yet. Sometimes I sweat it out over the first few weeks. But usually by the end of Week 2 getting out notebooks and writing will feel like "this is what we've always done."

Warm Up: What's on the Screen?

Action – groups of people or individuals (not necessarily human) doing something like fighting, rescuing kittens from trees, building a house, checking a pulse, and flying a spaceship. Look for images that suggest tension, conflict, intensity, and movement.

It's a good idea to post the same directions slide from Day 2. You might want to repeat the call and response from Day 2. But after that, take attendance or check everyone is started and then sit and write. This part is hard for teachers at first. It feels like we should be walking around actively proctoring. Resist the temptation to not write. I cannot stress how important not only this modeling is, but also the opportunity to develop your own writing is. You are building your habits too.

The sharing routine for writing warm up is almost always the same. Ask students to underline their favorite word, phrase, or sentence that they just wrote. Have them turn to a shoulder partner and read out loud what they underlined.

Mini-Lesson: Plot

Ask students to look at the pictures again and imagine what might have happened just before or just after the image was captured. If they get a good idea, they should jot that down. Explain or remind (depending on the age/experience of the writers) that the plot is what happens in a story. Character is who the story is about, plot is what happens. [Absolutely do not talk about the traditional plot diagram here. No. It's not relevant right now.]

Ask students if they think plot and action are the same thing and ask for examples from stories. Just like Day 2, with characters, students will offer a mix of movie and book plots, possibly video game plots as well. In general, plot and action might be the same thing. But some books have plots without a lot of action. Also, characters moving around doing things like opening a lemonade stand or trying out for the softball team are not necessarily action. Action implies a little more speed and intensity and often, higher stakes. A related question if you have a tiny bit more time for discussion is how much action is too much or too little? Kids definitely have opinions about this and it's interesting to hear their thinking and their examples. During the discussion part of the mini-lesson, teachers might use a variety of collaborative structures to facilitate increased participation. That being said, listening and jotting in one's notebook can be a great way to participate.

Post a list of possible plots and ask students to copy what they like and then add their own ideas. Just like Day 2 they're writing down plots that if they saw them on the back of a book, they would immediately want to read that book.

Grades 3–5

- Monsters on the loose

- Epic food fight

- Underdog sports team in the championship game

- Apprenticed to someone scary

- A regular day goes really wrong

Grades 6–8

- Reluctant hero on a quest

- Enemies who have to work together for _____ reason

- Secret identity causes problems

- Saving the world

- Revolution led by teens

- Last survivors of _____

Group students into 3's and 4's to share ideas and add to what they've written. Ask for highlights and try to hide your surprise at some of what might be shared. For example, one of the first times I did this lesson was with a group of 4th grade students at the beginning of the year. A student asked me, "What's the word for a demon in a box?" And I replied, "A dybbuk." Why I know that word, I couldn't say. But it was the word the student needed, and he wrote it down. Notice I didn't fan myself and say, "We don't talk about demons at school." But I made a mental note to check in during conferences to help the student stay within PG boundaries.

A 3rd -grade student declared her intent to write a story, "like *Lady and the Tramp*, but with pigs." "Yes," I responded. "I can't wait to read that!" Older students are sometimes less likely to share, but I've gotten a lot of murder, dystopian adventure, and sports ideas during this lesson.

Writers love story ideas. Ideas with interesting characters and interesting plots beg to be explored. As the facilitator of this conversation, try as much as possible to be in the idea/writing space of your brain. Shifting into the "I wouldn't want to read that" part of your brain will inadvertently send idea-suppressing signals to students. Teacher-pleasing students will want to write for their teacher, so try to like every single idea proposed. Students who are excited to capture a story idea are excited to write. That's the magic. These lists can and should grow over time as the developing writers become more aware of how plot shows up on book covers and in movie trailers.

Celebrate a successful putting away of notebooks routine.

Writer's Tools – Day 4

Warm-Up

Along with pictures of trees, vegetable or flower gardens, wildflowers, etc., post the question: Can you guarantee that seeds will grow?

Since a rule of the warm-up writing is that you don't have to write to the prompt, some students might ignore this question in favor of what they did on the previous days with plot and character. No worries. The important thing is that they're writing.

After completing the underline and share routine, explain that while writers have ideas all the time, some of those are ideas that, like seeds in the wrong soil, won't grow into a longer piece of writing. Many students are used to a strict *one idea:one piece of writing* ratio. Further, that one idea nearly always had to be finalized and polished. Professional writers have ideas all the time and all over the place. We can't publish them all. But we can play with and imagine and connect those ideas for fun.

Next, ask students to count all the words they've written this week and write the total under today's date. Celebrate as the numbers are called out. Not everyone will shout out their word count, but some will be pleasantly surprised.

Ask students what's working so far about the routines, what's been offered for choices, other thoughts? Ask about their notebooks, pencil/pens as well as desks, groups, etc. Be available for suggestions. For example, next week during the first Free Write Friday, students might be able to sit wherever in the room (or the hall if you're brave) they will be most productive.

Tonight for homework or tomorrow during class, students will complete a survey about the types of writing they want to learn.

Use a digital/Google form for this. Paper works too but you won't get a nice graph of the responses. Make sure to collect names if doing this electronically because this will be good information to refer back to later.

Questions for the survey:

1. Check all of the genres and topics that interest you:
   - Science fiction
   - Writing process strategies aka what to do when you're stuck
   - Fantasy
   - How a book gets published
   - Horror
   - Realistic contemporary
   - Historical
   - Romance
   - Fan fiction
   - Tools for writing an immersive setting
   - Mystery, suspense, thriller
   - Main plot versus sub-plot(s) and why more conflict is better
   - Sports
   - Humor
   - Narrative non-fiction
   - Improving dialog
   - Other
2. From the list above, please type your top three choices in order of preference (e.g., Thriller, More Conflict, Romance)

Ask Yourself

1. What do I need as a leader of this writing community?
2. What assumptions am I making about my students' experiences with writing?
3. Does our classroom configuration (desk arrangement, etc.) provide spaces for individual writing, conferring, and small group work?

When asked what they need to lead a writing community, teachers usually say something like, "a schedule." Or sometimes they say, "guidance" or "help." Schedules are good and help is great, but at the core of a writer leader's heart needs to be courage founded on the belief that these efforts will create positive outcomes for students. Teachers know that when they've committed to a course of action, their students can *feel* the iron-clad commitment and the forward motion will be smoother. When we are reluctant leaders, along the lines of "I think this X is stupid, but the administration says we have to X," our students respond with parallel reluctance. Throughout this journey, it is critical that teachers write along with students, trying every prompt, and every assignment as they are. Not only will this add to the deepening sense of community, but it will change the way you confer with your developing writers.

What you know about your students and their prior experiences with writing is dependent on many things such as the grade level you teach, vertical articulation in your school/school system, the percentage of transient students in your system, and so forth. I used to assume my students had mostly negative experiences or no substantive experiences with writing prior to my class. I always pre-assessed their writing, but I didn't always flat out ask about writing. Over time, my assumptions shifted to include my students having experiences with persuasive writing, and writing in response to reading, with the occasionally free write experience thrown into the mix.

Many of the conversations I have in high schools are about helping students figure out learning routines and procedures that work best for them in service to developing a set of portable study habits to take to college. These first two chapters serve the same purpose which is to provide student writers with a variety of experiences in writing to help them develop portable writing habits.

Just like the ceremony of getting out and putting away writer's notebooks, adjusting desk configuration for writing is important. Some writers prefer to sit on the floor, some prefer a desk. Some want to be as far away from others as possible, some want to be near friends, some need to look out a window. If you are able to add a rug and some pillows or a couch to your classroom, your student writers will be thrilled.

Furniture moving is something I didn't consider much except as a way to jazz up my seating chart. Then I watched a class moving the desks to set up a courtroom arrangement for a mock trial, how their behavior changed, how well they worked together, and the first kernel of an idea formed. Some of us are required to integrate movement and/or brain breaks into instructional time. Why not move the desks around? If you can't move your furniture, allowing the students to spread out and change seats still makes a difference. After practicing and gradual release, I can usually say, "go where you need to be" and my students find their best spots for writing. And I do too. I model this very purposefully. If I'm just playing around with ideas, I'm in a comfy chair with my writer's notebook. If I'm drafting or revising, I'm at a desk with a laptop.

Ask Your Students

1. What do you wish you knew how to write and why?
2. Think of a time when you enjoyed writing. What were you doing that worked? If this time was during school, please include what your teacher did that worked.
3. What do writers need to feel productive and successful?

All the savvy teachers know formative assessment is important. But asking your students about writing is just as important as collecting initial writing samples. Here's why – more than nearly any other subject, students claim to get stuck during writing and have no idea what to do next. (One could hazard a guess that this also happens in math, but most elementary classrooms have posters about what to do when you're stuck in math.) I'm not sure I've ever seen a chart or poster about what to do when you're stuck in your writing except in rare instances.

Where do student writers get stuck? Usually at or near the beginning of a piece. If you know their writing history, you have a much better chance of helping clear the block. For example, many students, especially 6th grade and older, come to us with what author and researcher Brené Brown calls creativity scars. Their writing was criticized for not being enough of what the teacher wanted, mocked because of the topic or genre they chose, or their style was flattened and squished into a tight, formulaic box. *Stuckness* can also be the first indicator of learned helplessness. Some students have learned that if they wait long enough, the teacher will rescue them with a plan, a plot, an opening paragraph, etc. Other students refuse to start because they're convinced their writing won't live up to the writer they most admire or their own artificial standards of what they should be able to do.

Later in this book, we'll spend time with mentor texts, but for this section, it's important to note that beginnings are difficult. Rather than try to write the perfect beginning, my advice is usually to start with the part that interests you the most and go from there. Later, during revision, is the time to think about words like "perfect" and "best."

Most students won't think of equipment right away when asked about what writers need to be successful, but pens, pencils, notebooks, and later, computers are essential. You will have to model this every day. In response to that third question about what writers need to feel successful, many students will say, "I don't know." Some will talk about a product they made, like a poetry anthology. Some will talk about a teacher who made writing fun. It is the rare student who answers this question as a writer, but I have had the pleasure of working with some of those individuals. They say things like, "plenty of time to write" and "being able to choose my own topics." What they don't know they need is **you**, a *writing* teacher. The students who already think of themselves as writers have been writing without anyone's help, in most cases, for years. Some gifted people show up that way. BUT, you can guide, mentor, provide resources, be a sounding board, and when needed, edit that one hundred thousand word novel your 6th-grade student just finished.

Next Steps

Next Steps for Struggling or Reluctant Writers

Be patient. Find success in small places. It may be the case that struggling writers are very good at helping pass out or collecting writer's notebooks. It may be that reluctant writers don't want to decorate or personalize their notebooks because of negative feelings about writing. Find other ways for these students to participate in the formation of writing routines in your classroom. Through words, tone, facial expression, and body language convey the message that you believe this person will write when they are ready.

Next Steps for Gifted Writers

Gifted writers may view this classroom stuff with skepticism or ignore it altogether. They didn't need routines and fancy notebooks before now, so why make a big deal? Some gifted writers who have been left alone to write aren't necessarily going to jump into your workshop when invited. Also, be patient with them, give them space to figure out how they want to participate. Another type of gifted writer will want the expert role and will want to tell you and the rest of the class how it's done. They've just sort of figured things out and they want to share, usually to be helpful. Your role is to reinforce that the purpose of this initial workshop work is to offer multiple pathways for writer success. You may need to have a private conversation with your gifted writers about how just like in math, we teach different methods of problem solving, so also in writing. It would be unfair (gifted kids like things to be fair) if we only teach one way to do writing. The other part of the private conversation is to encourage the gifted writer to consider additional options, methods, and topics. I usually begin with the "bigger toolbox" argument, which is related to the "just in case you might need it" argument. However, I don't force this issue beyond "that's what works for you, each person in our community needs the same opportunity to figure things out." As long as a gifted writer continues to produce writing, support whatever works for them.

Writing Community

When thinking about barriers, one doesn't often consider the absence of something as a barrier. But if you think of a barrier as something that prevents growth, then an intangible barrier to writing can be the absence of support systems and structures for writing to develop. Without these supports, students are less likely to feel safe and less likely to take risks while exploring writing. This chapter will discuss teacher and school-level actions that can create or strengthen the systems necessary for developing writers.

Writing is an art. To create art is to take personal risks. A critical first step in providing students the means to write is giving them a safe place to try and fail. Beliefs about what writing is and also about what writing is not are also fundamental needs. Spend some time asking yourself and your students, "Why do we write? What are all the reasons one might write besides doing it for school?"

In teaching school, most of us learned how to create a classroom community with rules and expectations supported through positive reinforcement. Use some of those same strategies to set up the writing community inside your classroom. One support to co-create with students in the first week is a chart or poster of **Writerly Activities**. My charts include actions like:

- Staring into space
- Doodling
- Reading
- Drafting

- Revising
- Conferring
- Research

In addition, place a chart or a reminder somewhere about *What to do During Writing Workshop If You're Not Sure What You Should Be Doing*:

- Look around and see what the class and the teacher are doing. Do that.
- Make sure you have your notebook and a pen/pencil.
- Check the screen or the board.
- Write.

The one thing it's always ok to do during writing workshop is to write. Because I write during the warm-up and the mini-lesson, my students need a lot of visual reminders about their options so that we don't disrupt each other's work.

Setting up the rough structure of a writing community takes about a week or around five 45-minute practice opportunities. Third graders, at least at first, should probably work in 20–30 minute chunks. This is also true for 4th graders at the beginning of the year. But by mid-year, 4th graders can comfortably spend 45 minutes (or even longer) on writing. With older middle school students, you will also need to build in some "why are we doing this" moments. The time of year and expectations in your building will also shape how much of the *why* you need to front load. For these students, I always highlight the three types of writing outlined in the standards (Narrative, Informational, and Persuasive) and how these routines that we're developing will help us with all three. Eighth graders, in particular, need to be reassured that this writing, all the writing, will help them be ready for high school.

Writing Community – Lesson Ideas

Day 1 Everyone's from Somewhere – Setting

Warm-Up

Post images of interesting places and places that look like your community. Ask students to choose one place and describe it using all five senses. Remind them that smell is often overlooked by writers and yet is incredibly important. Even, or especially if, the smells are gross, they should try and describe them as part of describing this place.

Mini-Lesson – Setting as Point of View

After the sharing routine (underline your favorite word, phrase, or sentence, turn and share), ask students to make a t-chart on a new notebook page.

Show a picture of your school on the screen.

One side of the t-chart is labeled "Why _____ is great" and the other side is labeled "Why _____ is terrible." Explain that they are going to jot down aspects and characteristics of the school that they would talk up if they had a friend/cousin – someone they *liked* considering enrolling in one column. And in the other column, they will jot down aspects and characteristics of the school they would emphasize if a frenemy or someone they *disliked* wanted to enroll. The caveat? Everything jotted down has to be true.

This activity gets giggles and writers looking at each other and shifting around in their seats. Let everyone try for at least a few minutes. Then ask, "Is it possible that what might seem like a great thing to one prospective student might seem terrible to a different prospective student?" For example, what about a school where all the adults know your name? Some people might love this and feel included in the community. But other people might feel watched and confined. Another example might be lots of windows. Some students might hate the bright light early in the day and the glare on their desks as well as the potential for drafty cold air or extra heat (depending on the climate). Other students would love the natural light and how it helps them feel awake as well as the open feeling in rooms and halls with lots of window versus the cold, dark feeling of enclosed spaces.

Next ask, "How does the setting impact the story and the characters in the story? Would that be different for different characters?"

Show a few extreme and imaginary settings such as an underwater city, a castle at the top of a mountain, a massive spaceship, and ask students to choose one. They should jot down all the potential problems of that setting and then all the potentially awesome things about that setting. After that, they should jot a list of potential characters that might be found in that setting.

Give students some time to turn and talk or share in small groups. Call them back by asking if anyone is getting story ideas as they think about places. For the last few minutes, students can either continue their setting writing, or they can go back to their character and plot work from last week.

Writing Community

Day 2 – The Gift of a Stupid Idea

Warm-up

Once students are seated with notebooks and ready to go, play the clip from *The Lego Movie* (Lord, Phil, et al. *The LEGO Movie*. Warner Bros., 2014) where Emmet talks about his best idea. Search "Lego Movie Double Decker Couch" and choose videos. *As of this writing, several options for that clip are available on YouTube.*

In the first Lego movie, the main character, Emmet, is asked if he's ever had an original idea. It's a high-pressure moment for Emmet and he wants to impress the people who are asking. So he shows them his idea for a double-decker couch. The response is overwhelmingly negative. They are mean about it. One character says, "That's just the worst." The purpose of showing this to illustrate what **not** to do when a fellow writer shares their writing with you.

Explain that it's important to practice how to have a peer conference with another writer. The scene from *The Lego Movie* shows the wrong way. Ask for two volunteers to show a better way to respond to a fellow writer. Ask for two volunteers to show another positive, constructive option. Highlight choices like listening, nodding, asking questions, paraphrasing, etc. What students come up with on their own will vary by age and experience so jump in and offer suggestions if necessary.

Besides being an example of what not to do, what's good about this movie clip is that you can show the follow-up scene later in the film where the main characters are saved from drowning by the double-decker couch. Vindication of the "stupid" idea!

I also love taking one of the key themes from *The Lego Movie* – which is the goal of becoming a master builder – and using it as an analogy for writing. Once you know all the pieces and how they work, you can make anything in your imagination.

After the clip and the role play, invite students to list as many bad ideas for stories as they can. Have them star the best-worst idea and their worst-worst idea. Then invite them to practice sharing best and worst ideas in a mini-writing conference with a peer.

Writing Community

Day 3 – Ordinary People are Never Really Ordinary

Warm-up

Show pictures of people around the world engaged in mundane, daily activities. The prompt is: *Choose one of these people and imagine what makes them unique compared to the other people in the photo and unique compared to other people who farm/build skyscrapers/work in offices/cook in restaurants.*

Continue the routine of writing for five minutes and sharing a favorite word/phrase with a shoulder partner. Inevitably, someone will ask about sharing with the whole class again. I have a range of responses to this depending on where the class is as a community. One response is that we will have more formal sharing once we've completed and polished a full piece, but that won't happen for a while. Another response is "maybe on Friday."

*SEL note – for students who don't like to speak in front of the class and students who don't like to take risks or be wrong, sharing writing out loud to the whole group sounds terrible, possibly terrifying. Once you're ready to include some sharing routines, be sure to speak one-on-one with those students to help them find a comfortable option.

Mini-Lesson

On a fresh page in their notebook, ask students to list some of their favorite main characters, who are more or less "ordinary people" from books, movies, and television. The goal is to list at least five, but ten is better. For example, Meg, from *A Wrinkle in Time* (L'Engle, Madeleine. 1st ed. Ariel Books, 1962.) is a well-developed main character. She is a smart, ordinary girl drawn into an extraordinary adventure. This is a good time to do a table-sharing or small group sharing strategy to get a few more ideas into the room. Encourage students to add other's ideas into their notebooks and make sure to model that as you're walking around.

The next step is for everyone to circle their favorite character from their lists. They might also consider options from last week's character lists. Once everyone has a character in mind, introduce the character interview (see below for sample questions). You will need to model this for the whole group with a character either from your own list or from a story you are currently writing. I usually model with something from my own writing and explain that the character interview is a tool that really helps me both when I'm getting started on a new project and when I'm feeling stuck.

Give your students the same choice. They can complete a character interview using a known character from someone else's work. OR they can complete a character interview using a character from their own imaginations.

A character interview is what I call a "writerly activity." It's not actually writing but it is something writers do as part of the story creation process. Encourage students to take time with these questions as they will use the answers throughout the story they might write. Encourage students to notice where this type of character information is showing up in their mentor texts and independent reading.

*Sample Character Interview Questions:

Name:
Age:
Physical description:
Cultural background (including languages spoken):
What are they good at? Special skills or abilities?
What do they love to do?
Describe this character's family. Do they get along?
Where do they live? What's it like there?
What does this character keep in their pockets, purse, backpack, bag, etc.?
Does this character hide any of their stuff? If so, where?
Any favorites? (Colors, places, people, animals, etc.)
What kinds of things make this character happy?
What makes this character annoyed or upset?
Who does this character admire and why?
Three words to describe this character:
What are this character's negative traits?
How does this character speak? (Quickly, slowly, lots of jokes, sarcastic, interrupts)

What is this character's happiest memory?
*adapted from YWP NANOWRIMO Young Novelist Workbook (*NaNoWriMo's Young Writers Program*, ywp.nanowrimo.org/pages/writer-resources.)

Free Write Friday! Yes!

Free Write Friday's routine goes like this: "Look through your notebook at all the bits and pieces of this you wrote so far this week. Pick at least one or even a few to expand. Try to write at least 100 words but shoot for 300 words. We're going to write for 30 minutes." Point to the chart you made about writerly activities and remind students that these things are also options except for conferring with peers. Today is their time to confer with you. Teachers have many ways of handling writing conferences. I usually have an open list on a clipboard as well as my own class list to make sure I'm conferring with each student every two weeks.

The big routine change is that on Fridays the teacher doesn't write. This is your time to meet with students about their writing. On the first Free Write Friday, students might start to get restless at the 20-minute mark. If so, just stop early and try for 25 minutes next Friday. With practice and support, most students can work toward 45 minutes of silent, sustained writing each week. *I see your skeptical face, but this is truth born from hundreds of hours of trial and error. Try it and let me know.*

Free Write Friday is incredibly important for several reasons. Chief among those is that it builds writing stamina. Every student needs the opportunity to experience the success of writing for a long period of time. Later when you get into other types of writing, you will be so glad you've given your students this skill set. Another reason is that you are all writing together as a writing community. Just like other community norms, Free Write Friday sustains and protects itself because it becomes a valued activity. Finally, Free Write Friday is self-directed writing. Again, depending on the experiences your students have had prior to this, they may never have directed their own writing. In the early weeks of writing work, I find myself repeating, "I don't really care what you write as long as it's okay for school." Many teachers have adopted this stance about reading. They just want kids to read and love reading. Far fewer teachers have thought to be as open about student writing choices.

After notebooks are safely away, have a small treat for each student, like an individually wrapped piece of candy. Congratulations!

Conferring

Each Friday try to meet with five to seven students for about five minutes each. Keep track of who you're meeting with and make notes somewhere you can find again. [I use a clipboard and then transfer the notes to a table/spreadsheet.] Some teachers work their way through the alphabet, some have students put their names on the board to request a conference on Free Write Friday. Teachers can/will confer with students on other days during writing practice, but Friday is the largest chunk of time available.

Some students are excellent at not conferring and avoiding talking about writing. This doesn't mean they aren't writing, but it might. That's why keeping track is important. Other students would rather confer than write. For this reason, some teachers also track and manage minutes spent in peer conferences. Gentle reminders like, "talking about writing is not the same as writing," sometimes help redirect the students who are more social thinkers.

Should you do a model writing conference so students know what to expect? Probably. Probably yes. Skipping this is like skipping teaching routines. But every year and every class is different. Do what works.

Sometimes I have a student who is a natural, confident writer model a conference with me, after we've practiced quietly together, and the student is comfortable. Other times, I model a conference with another adult. Depending on the situation, I have been both "the writer" and "the teacher." Middle school students respond well when I'm "the writer" in the modeled conference. They truly enjoy asking me pointed questions and giving me advice on how to improve my writing.

Possible Model Conference Script

Student as "the teacher": What are you thinking about writing so far this year?

Me as "the writer": It's pretty good.

Student/the teacher: What do you have in your notebook that you're working on?

Me/the writer: *points to page in notebook* I have this one about a monster. *turns page* And this one about my dog.

Student/the teacher: How many words do you have so far?

Me/the writer: 451

Student/the teacher: That's great! What question did you want to talk about?

Me/the writer: *glances at chart of questions* Um, I was wondering about the setting with the monster. Like, should it be in the human world? Or the monster world?

Student/teacher: *holds out hands for notebook* *skims page* Okay, so here is a sentence about where the monster lives. And down here is a sentence about how cold it is there. And that's why the monster wants to come to the human world?

Me/the writer: *nods*

Student/teacher: What's the main problem of the story? That the monster is unhappy?

Me/the writer: I'm not sure.

Student/teacher: Okay, well, the setting should be where the main problem is. Like, spend the most words on describing the place where the main problem takes place. Do you need help thinking about the main problem?

Me/the writer: Not right now.

Student/the teacher: Let me know. I think this will be a fun story to read when it's finished. Keep writing, you have a great start! I'll check in with you next week.

Me/the writer: Okay

In the first month of conferring I ask students to bring between 100–300 words of a current piece and one question with them to the conference. These are the same questions I suggest they use to begin writing conferences with peers. Post sample questions such as:

- Does the dialog sound like how real people talk?
- In what ways do the characters seem authentic and true to_____ (whatever they are humans, dragons, vampires)?
- What aspects of the setting need more/less explanation?
- How is the balance between description and action?
- How could I expand this scene?
- Is the flow of the story working?

When we're brainstorming what might be good questions to ask in a writing conference, I say, "What you want to ask, what all writers want to ask is, 'Is it good?' And 'Do you like it?'" But those questions don't have helpful answers. During conferences, the questions have to be about the writing and how the writing is progressing. That's being said, I always try to express genuine enthusiasm or curiosity about *the idea* the student is working on. Validation about ideas helps student writers press forward when the writing feels hard and the words are slowly getting to the page. One of my best writing friends will sometimes say, "I can't wait until this story is out in the world." Just that little touch of positivity makes a huge difference.

Ask Yourself

Does my classroom community have what it needs to support a robust writer's workshop? Do I have norms in place for what students can do if they can't talk directly to me during work time? Am I willing to write every day alongside my students? Am I willing to take the same risks I'm asking my students to take?

You might have your own creativity scars from early or more recent school years. Those don't necessarily fade with writing time. Or, you might have been neutral about writing and now, as you attempt writing with your students, imposter syndrome may creep in.

All writers feel these sorts of feelings.

In the early days of my first novel, a person I'd met at a conference and I exchanged manuscripts to critique each other. When we met to share feedback, he turned to a section and asked me something like, "Did you add this point of view just so you could info dump this stuff here?"

Much to my embarrassment, I realized, yes, that was exactly what I'd done. Which I admitted. But here's the important part. He patted the pages in front of him and said, "I understand. I'm a writer too." Your students need this sense of community and camaraderie with you. And honestly, you might need it from them.

The other thing you might ask yourself, related to what you're asking students, is how much writing in our community is about learning versus how much is about practicing? Ask yourself how much writing you do in your own life and would you be willing to try new things? To write more words and with more frequency?

You might have that feeling when you're trying to follow a recipe for the first time, and you forgot to check how much cumin you have and whether or not you have the right set of measuring spoons or enough olive oil.

> I kind of hate that feeling.
> But I love the feeling of perfecting a recipe after 2-3 tries.
> Are you cooking for the Queen? Or a famous food critic? No.

Some teachers resist writing with students and pushing themselves into that uncomfortable emotional space because they have thoughts related to perfection like they're writing for the New York Times book review. But you're not writing for anyone fancy, you're writing to sustain yourself and please yourself. Just as you're cooking for yourself and possibly your family to sustain them and please them, on the successful recipe days.

Ask Your Students

At the end of this week, ask students to write down what their goals are in terms of how they hope to grow as writers this year. Have them put a big star by their goal or goals in their notebooks. They will be checking on their goals, possibly adding to them or changing them as the year unfolds.

When my older daughter was in elementary school, I asked her, "What is the purpose of reading?" This was a child who was a blazing fast fiction reader and miles above grade level but hated non-fiction unless it had a lot of pictures. She paused longer than usual and finally said, "To learn."

Using whatever large group discussion routine you like best, ask your students, "What are all the reasons *a person* might write?" The first response may be something like, "The teacher made us." Or a variation, "For an assignment." You might nudge them toward, "Birthday cards" "Hello to my Grandmother" "So I don't forget to do something" The next nudge might get the group to "To reflect on something that happened." Or "To get my feelings down on paper."

Once they've reached their level of tolerance for open responses, change the question and ask, "What are all the reasons *a writer* might write?" Now you will get responses like, "To tell a story" and "To use their imagination" or "To be silly" or "To scare people" you might get "to make money" or "it's their job."

You might follow up with, "Does writing out an idea help you think about it?" Or "Can writing be a part of learning?"

Here's a secret that writers know: The only way to learn how to write [a book, a poem, a news story] is to write. Therefore, writing is learning.

For your gifted students, you're nudging them toward the idea of creating something new that's never been in the world before. Working at the highest level of Bloom's Taxonomy is required to write well, whether it's fiction or non-fiction. For your struggling and reluctant writers, you're gently expanding their ideas about the usefulness of writing and the wide range of options for writing.

Ask "What do people need to feel safe to learn?" And "What do writers need to feel safe to learn?" My teaching philosophy has always been about co-creating the learning community with my students. I tend to overuse the pronouns *Our* and *We*, especially at the beginning of the year. Even when I think I've done a pretty good job, my students will let me know what's missing and what they need. Bottom line, the classroom and within that, the writing community, needs to be a place where each student feels safe and supported to challenge themselves and grow.

Next Steps

Next Steps for Gifted Writers

Some gifted writers will begin to relax and trust the routines and community at the end of these two weeks. Some gifted writers might need more time. Regardless of the system you've devised for conferring, consider meeting with gifted writers sooner rather than later, especially the ones who still appear closed and reluctant. For the gifted writers who are ready to grow, find out which writing craft books they have/have read. Spend a bit more time talking about both their mentor authors and their goals for themselves.

For gifted writers who already have a WIP (writer shorthand for Work in Progress), invite them to try the sample character interview with one of their own characters. The entire resource book for the Young Writers Program from NaNoWriMo, might also be what they're ready for. It's free online at https://ywp.nanowrimo.org/pages/writer-resources.

Next Steps for Struggling or Reluctant Writers

For your students who are not sure they want to write, or for whom writing is a significant challenge, provide ways to see small, incremental success. For some students writing a single sentence during class is a victory. Keep plenty of sticky notes handy for these students because at first, a whole notebook page might feel overwhelming. Instead, they can "fill" a 3×3 sticky note with a single cool idea. Sometimes these students move to a larger sticky note or an index card before they move to a notebook page. Make sure to have some of your own short writing taped into your writer's notebook as a model.

Be prepared to accept as many ideas as you can. Say "yes" to your reluctant writers' story ideas because as long as what they're writing is ok for school, it's all good. One of my highly capable but non-producing writers started a story about a duck and a goose that he thought was hilarious. He wrote five installments of that story over the course of a quarter and later his parent told me it was the most he'd written in a long time. It is hard to resist the urge to coach at this moment and to encourage the writer to "do more at grade level." Keep reminding yourself this is the community building stage and that your acceptance of wild and sometimes easy-silly ideas will pay off down the road.

The Motivation to Write – Write What You Want to Read

Fantasy, Crime, and Science Fiction

Choice is an incredibly powerful tool. The chapters in this section contain the how's and why's of teaching various fiction genres to writers who are suddenly interested in what the teacher has to show them. And where does the sudden interest come from?

Students Want to Learn How to Write What They Love to Read

They have a suspicion that there must be a way to learn how Brandon Sanderson does what he does, or Jason Reynolds, or Marie Lu. But schools rarely explore the exotic worlds of writing genre fiction, and in forgoing those explorations, cost the world so many potential writers.

Often in frontloading, a single concept or piece of vocabulary can unlock understanding. And if one word can unlock understanding about the underlying structure of genre fiction, it's the word TROPE. I still remember the first time I heard "trope" bantered around by a group of writers and having that dawning feeling of "why did I not know this?"

As an itinerant teacher and specialist, I get to do short- and long-term writing projects in other people's classrooms. The first lesson I usually teach is about tropes. Brains like novelty and students like learning something that feels cool, unique, and outside the norm. During the tropes lesson, I model my deep and nerdy love for all things genre fiction and I make my pitch that this is a very fun kind of fiction to write. Tropes are there to help set expectations and structure the story process. This lesson also provides an overview of character, setting, and plot, through the lens of tropes.

Young adult examples:

- I used to hate you and now I want to date you = Romance Plot Trope.
- Super awkward new kid = Humor Character Trope.
- Creepy abandoned hospital = Horror Setting Trope.

Middle grade examples:

- Going on a quest = Fantasy Plot Trope.
- Wise and inspirational coach = Sports Character Trope.
- Specialized museum/bank vault in an exotic location = Crime Setting Trope.

Since character, plot, and setting were introduced during the Writing Community lessons, don't spend precious time on additional mini-lessons about those topics in isolation. Every single genre fiction lesson reinforces these three concepts in an integrated way. Also, don't worry if you or your students don't master the concept of tropes on your first pass through, the understanding comes with practice and application.

Mini-Lesson – Tropes

Search for the Geico commercial featuring the people who are in a horror movie. The tag line "When you're in a horror movie, you make poor decisions. It's what you do." Plus "Geico" will find the video on YouTube. (Geico. "When You're in a Horror Movie." Sept. 2014.)

Give a definition of the word tropes before you play the video. Here's a good one from tvtropes.org.

> A trope is a storytelling device or convention, a shortcut for describing situations the storyteller can reasonably assume the audience will recognize. Tropes are the means by which a story is told by anyone who has a story to tell. Tropes may be brand new but seem trite and hackneyed; they may be thousands of years old but seem fresh and new. They are not bad; they are not good. They are simply tools that a creator of a work of art uses to express their ideas to the audience.

In short, a trope is about expectations. While watching a horror movie, you expect the characters to make poor decisions. Show the Geico commercial and walk students through the two main horror tropes shown:

The prettiest person is the dumbest – so when the blonde girl asks, "Why don't we get in the running car?" it's the worst idea – because in horror movie logic, *bad decisions are good and good decisions are wrong*.

The attic? The basement? No, the worst idea is to "hide behind the chainsaws." Even the scary-looking guy in the garage is shaking his head at them.

Finally, as the Geico tagline ends, one character says, "Quick head for the cemetery!"

Does it ruin anyone's fun to know the tropes/expectations ahead of time? No. Tropes are like lane lines for writers, just there to keep the story on track and within the genre.

Every genre has plot, character, and setting tropes. Again, you can substitute the word expectations for trope.

Next show the ad for a "murder by mail" product called "Post Mortem." (Mysterious Package Company. "LA: Lights, Camera, Murder!" Mysterious Package Company, Dec. 2018, mysteriouspackage.com/products/post-mortem-la-lights-camera-murder.) This is set up like a 50's detective show. Ask students to watch and ask them to be ready to share what they expected to see. [If you can't find this, show the season 1 trailer for the original *CSI* or *Castle*.] They should call out: a crime scene, detectives, people photographing evidence, weapon, etc.

People who like a certain genre, like crime shows, hope, and expect to see these things. So when a writer decides to write crime fiction, they need to include at least some of those tropes to meet the readers' expectations.

- Bruckheimer, Jerry. Season CSI: Crime Scene Investigators, episode Season 1 Trailer, Sept. 2000.

- Beacon Pictures, and ABC Studios. Season Castle, episode Season 1 Trailer, Feb. 2009.

Incidentally, a book cannot be shelved in the mystery section of the bookstore if the mystery isn't solved. And a book cannot be shelved in the romance section if it doesn't have a happy ending. In both these cases, genre expectations have become publishing requirements.

Create slides using the following. Each is meant to contain examples of some of the most common tropes, not present a complete list. This is just a taste of tropey goodness to whet students' appetites for all the genre fiction to come.

Talk through each of the slides, checking for understanding as needed. Students can jot these down as written OR you can ask for book/film/game examples of these tropes, First up, Science Fiction."

- Alien Invasion
- Computer Virus – EMP
- Colonization
- Ark Ship
- Zombie Apocalypse
- Superheroes/Mutants
- Dystopia/Utopia

Plot/Character tropes from Fantasy – Put this on a separate slide

The first two on this list, quest and "the one" are uber tropes in fantasy and we see them ALL. THE. TIME. Students should be able to think of plenty of examples.

- Sent on a Quest
- The ONE who will save us
- Royalty in Disguise
- Curse
- Magic that will_____

Next slide – examples of Crime Fiction character tropes:

- Amateur Sleuth
- Private Investigator

- Professional (CIA, MI5, NSA, Interpol, etc.)
- Ex-professional (former Navy Seal, former police officer, etc.)

Next slide - examples of Crime Fiction plot tropes:

Absence of evidence, beneath suspicion, the butler did it, eagle eye detection, evidence scavenger hunt, evil plan, finger-licking poison, hidden in plain sight, lights off – somebody dies, ripped from the headlines, stakeout, you meddling kids, etc.

Use a different image for each slide. By the time you arrive at crime fiction plot tropes, the students are beginning to get the idea. *Trope* is a key vocabulary word for the next 9 weeks. Today is just the introduction.

Writing Practice

Ask students to think about their favorite books/movies/games and the tropes they most enjoy. Have them start a list of the tropes they might want to incorporate like *fake dating* or *lonely kid has hidden powers*. Remind students [and yourself] that you will be practicing with tropes a lot and not to worry if they're kind of uncertain about them at first.

PDF's of the slide decks I use, with copyrighted material removed, are available as online supplemental materials with this book. My recommendation is that you work on a genre a week. The decks can be broken down into about three mini-lesson. Each gives you lots of flexibility to frame these inside your normal literacy block and leaves room for Free-Write Friday/Conferring.

Resist the temptation to stretch any genre past a week, at least this first time through your students' interests. Quicker pacing will please your fast learners as well as those with short attention spans. Also, in case you have one or two students in your group who "hate" a particular genre, you can assure them we only have about three mini-lessons for each one. Generally, I find haters relax their stance as we peel back the layers of each genre, revealing the full range of writing options. But staying in motion helps too.

Lesson Ideas – Fantasy

Fantasy – Day 1

Learning how to write Fantasy is the #1 top choice of student writers with few exceptions. Grades 3–8 pick Fantasy as their first genre to study 95% of the time.

Overview + Creatures

On the first day of teaching a new genre, offer a definition. For example:

> Fantasy, as a genre of fiction, usually takes place in imaginary worlds or our world, but not as we know it. Fantasy characters, which may or may not be human, often have magic or are magical.

Warm-Up

Use images of creatures from mythology or fantasy and a simple prompt like, "Choose one of these creatures to describe for your warm-up today." Change these out depending on the time of year, but try to include elves, witches, mermaids, centaurs, ghosts, and werewolves.

Brainstorm Mentor Texts

Use covers or posters or other types of images of a few books, films, television shows, and games to get them started, and then give the students 90 seconds to list as many as books, movies, etc., that are classified as Fantasy. Remind them that the key difference between Fantasy and Science Fiction is that in Fantasy, magic/people cause the main problems. In Science Fiction, science/people cause the main problems.

When time is up use whatever group strategy you like to have students share out their lists. My rule is that an idea can't be repeated. If one person says, "Harry Potter and the Prisoner of Azkaban" (Rowling, J.K., Scholastic, 1999) other people can't say any of the other *Harry Potter* titles. Even if you are the most connected teacher with a deep knowledge of past and current pop culture, you won't know all the things like the students name. That's fine. Just ask, "what causes the main problem?" I accept all answers except the ones I know for sure are not fantasy. Table 3.1, at the end of this section, contains a short list of strong mentor texts to offer students.

Mini-Lesson

Show a list of possible fantasy creatures: Elves, Trolls, Dwarves, Witches/Warlocks/Wizards, Fairies, Dragons, Vampires, Werewolves, Mermaids, Giants, Unicorns, and Ghosts. Explain that one of the gifts of writing Fantasy is the amazing wealth of choices found in ancient and contemporary mythology from around the world.

Students choose one from the list, or pick a different option based on their interests or a mentor text (for example, someone might choose Cyclops because they love Percy Jackson's half-brother, Tyson). Readers first meet Tyson in book 2 of the Percy Jackson series, *The Sea of Monsters*. (Riordan, Rick. Disney/Hyperion Books, 2014) For now, take "human" off the table as an option, even though humans are often creatures found in fantasy stories.

In their notebooks, have students draw, write, and/or make notes about the following, regarding the creature they chose:

- Physical description
- Clothing/wardrobe (not applicable for all creatures)
- Strengths (skills, powers)
- Weaknesses
- General personality traits
- Origins - specific place? How created?
- Does this creature have magic? If yes, how does it work?
- Are special skills or weapons needed to defeat or kill this creature?

Example – Ghost

> **Physical description:** *Semi-transparent, otherwise human-looking.*
> **Clothing:** *Whatever the person was wearing when they died, except in rare exceptions if ghost can change its appearance.*

Strengths: *Can travel in both spirit realm and human realm, can inspire a sense of dread, can lower the perceived temperature in a room, can interact with objects (shatter glass, slam doors) in some instances.*

Weaknesses: *Salt, iron, sunrise.*

General personality traits: *In some cases, ghosts retain the personality they had in life, in other cases the ghost is stuck in the most powerful emotion retained at the moment of death usually anger or fear. Some ghosts are helpful. Some are possessive of a certain object or location. Some are vengeful.*

Origins: *Unresolved death/cause of death, grave disturbed, occasionally ghosts rise due to certain types of spells.*

Does this creature have magic? *Not exactly, but the ability to move between planes or realms can seem like magic.*

Are special skills or weapons needed to defeat this creature? *This depends on the type of story and the cultural context of the story. Often simple means will work such as resolving the cause of death or releasing the spirit's bindings to a particular place or object.*

Scaffold – have a few partially filled out, using sentence frames as needed. Extension – ask the students to note which cannon or cultural mythology their creature is connected to, e.g., demons in Korean mythology are quite different from demons from the American South.

Once everyone has the basics drawn, written, and/or listed, invite students to think about how a creature is introduced in Fantasy. Show a few examples from popular fiction, such as *The Fellowship of the Ring* (Tolkien, J. R. R. 1st ed., George Allen & Unwin, 1954) or *Children of Blood and Bone* (Adeyemi, Tomi. Henry Holt and Company, 2018). All the Rick Riordan books have creatures if those are easier to find in the school library. Locate the few sentences where the author brings the creature to the page and shows the reader what that creature can do, the role it might play in the story, etc.

Invite the students to write something along those lines for the creature they've just invented. Provide a set of character introduction choices such as:

- This creature arrives and turns the tide in the battle.
- This creature is hiding and wounded and needs help.

- Someone accidentally discovers this creature in its secret home.
- A magical object (ring, lamp, trumpet) causes this creature to appear.
- This creature loses its disguise in the middle of a crowd of humans.

Scaffold – some students may need to do this as a story board or a few comic panels with only a few words under each.
Extension – some students may be ready to turn this into a full scene including action and dialog.

Ask students to think about their new creature through the lens of tropes. Could their creature be any of the following Fantasy character tropes?

- Royalty in Disguise
- The Chosen One
- Secret Heir
- Evil Overlord
- The Lucky Novice
- Godparent who grants wishes

Close this lesson with a quick round-up of Humans in Fantasy: may or may not be the main character(s), may or may not have magic, may or may not be from that world. Ask students to add other ideas about how humans tend to be represented in Fantasy novels.

The next lesson is about world-building, which will include thinking about how magic works. (This is better anticipatory set if you put up an interesting picture.)

Fantasy Day 2 – World-Building*

Several years ago, I attended a fantasy world-building session at a writing conference. Our presenter had us start by drawing a map. At first I was like, "Oh no, I can't draw!" But when the presenter's model looked like a circle covered by assorted jelly bean shapes I realized this wasn't art class, it was geography class.

Geography, including available water for crops, timber or stone or mud for structures, and natural barriers like mountains, contributes to how societies evolve and interact with each other.

Until that session, I'd thought the map at the front of a given fantasy novel was for reference only. Now I understand those maps can show the writer where the story starts.

This would be a great lesson to co-teach with your next door social studies teacher or to connect to your current geography/history unit. All the questions and ideas below (with the exceptions of creatures and magic) can be illustrated by various moments in our planet's history.

Warm-Up

Today's opener for writing should be a map – I often use a medieval map I found online that has the dragons on the borders to signify that dragons lived on the edges of the known world. The writing question is: *Imagine you're an explorer tasked with confirming the existence of dragons. Write down your observations as you get closer to the farthest point covered in your map.*

Explain that the very broad genre called fantasy has many sub-genres. The world-building in this lesson applies to all of them, except Urban Fantasy that uses the known world as a template over which is laid some form of magic, magical creatures, etc. *The Lightning Thief* by Rick Riordan (Riordan, Rick. Miramax Books/Hyperion Books for Children, 2005.) is a great exemplar because Riordan takes the time to explain the location/ geography of Camp Half-Blood, Mount Olympus, and the Underworld. An avid fan could take a map of the US and fill in where "the mist" is working to conceal the existence of people and creatures of mythology from ordinary humans. Depending on the age of my students, I also like to call out the *Shadow Hunters* series by Cassandra Clare that begins with *City of Bones* (Clare, Cassandra. Margaret K. McElderry Books, 2010) as an exemplar of urban fantasy.

Mini-Lesson – World-Building

Step 1

Draw a map (this step can take anywhere from 5–30 minutes depending on the students. If map-making takes most of the writing time for the day, it's fine to break world-building into two classes.)

Include: Mountains, Forests, Rivers, Oceans, Plains, Towns, and if applicable, Cities

Step 2

Determine the rules of this world specific to:

(As students are thinking about rules, they can jot their ideas on the map or in their notebooks.)

- Magic – Who has it? Who doesn't? How does it work? Does using magic have a price?
- Languages – Many languages spoken? Only one language?
- Education – does formal school exist? Who has access to education? Does this world use apprenticeships or other alternative methods of teaching?
- Trade – given the geography of this world, certain regions will have more of some resources and less of others. How does trade happen? Is it regulated by a government? Do the societies in this world use a form of money? Or is everything bartered?

Step 3

Creatures – Students should definitely consider using the creatures they worked on in the previous lesson.

- What types of creatures occupy the different regions of this world?
- Do humans live in this world?
- Do some humans have additional abilities, e.g., magic?
- Do the groups of creatures, humans, and humans-with-abilities get along?

Step 4

Systems (this is an advanced/optional step)

- Do larger systems create structure across this world?
- Examples of systems:

- Magic
- Religious
- Political
- Economic
- Social

A great example of a unique magical system is in *The Amulet of Samarkand* by Jonathan Stroud (Hyperion Books For Children, 2003.). In this book, magicians don't have their own magic. They steal it from the captured *djinn*.

Once the skeleton of the new world is built, writers can decide what stories jump out and clamor to be written. Professional writers sometimes call these ideas "plot bunnies." Use the following as examples of story ideas that might come from what's on the map:

- Elves have a shaky alliance with dwarves to protect secret mines.
- Rumors abound that the dragons are now extinct. But the main character needs the help of a dragon in order to_____.
- Danger awaits on all sides of the peaceful farming town.
- Bandits using illegal dark magic disrupt trade between the two largest cities on X continent.

This is a very sneaky way of planning. I generally don't even mention that writers do this to plan since many of my students claim to be allergic to planning. What I love about this activity is that it anchors story creation in something tangible. Not sure what happens next? Let's look at your map. Not sure how long that journey would take two trolls and a human? Let's look at your map.

Fantasy Day 3 – Going on an Adventure & How the Fantasy Genre Intersects with the Hero's Journey

Warm-Up

Choose a few images of people doing something risky, like mountain climbing, or images of people engaged in combat, like a medieval battle or fencing. Ask, "What are these characters doing and why? How would magic change the situation?"

Mini-Lesson

Now that the writers have a sense of what creatures will inhabit their fantasy stories and where the main action will take place in their fantasy worlds, they need to decide on an overarching story problem, aka, plot.

The most common fantasy plots involve going on a quest or going on an adventure.

Other common Fantasy plot tropes:

- A curse
- Magic that will_____.
- Powerful artifact
- Lurking evil
- Forbidden:
    - Forest
    - Castle
    - Land
    - Ally
    - Love interest

In adventure fiction, specifically, stories that follow the Hero's Journey plot structure, the main character falls into two distinct categories. Half of our heroes choose the adventure, the other half have the adventure forced on them. I use Bilbo, from *The Hobbit* and Frodo, from *The Fellowship of the Ring,* to illustrate this difference. Bilbo is tricked into the adventure. Frodo has been so ready to leave the Shire. Shrek, in the first film, has the adventure/quest forced on him in order to get his swamp back. Lucy, in *The Lion, the Witch, and The Wardrobe*, is bored and looking for an adventure. She chooses to help Mr. Tumnus. And so on. You don't necessarily want to spend a lot of class time discussing these examples, but your students with a deep knowledge of fantasy novels and films, they may want to make a chart or poster. One of my favorite film adaptations is *Treasure Planet*, adapted from the classic *Treasure Island* by Robert Louis Stevenson. When I'm teaching this lesson, I show the theatrical trailer for *Treasure Planet* and ask the students to look for the adventure tropes.

Tolkien, J. R. R. The Hobbit. 1st ed., George Allen & Unwin, 1937.

Tolkien, J. R. R. The Fellowship of the Ring. 1st ed., George Allen & Unwin, 1954.

Adamson, Andrew and Vicky Jenson, directors. Shrek. Dreamworks, 2001.

Lewis, C. S. The Lion, the Witch and the Wardrobe. 1st ed., Geoffry Bles, 1950.

Stevenson, Robert Louis. *Treasure Island*. London: Cassell and Company, 1883.

Musker, John, and Ron Clements. *Treasure Planet*. Walt Disney Pictures, 2002.

Quests are taken/given for a variety of reasons. Some common quests students might want to play with for their main story problems:

- Find a person who is missing/lost.
- Find a person who is missing AND has key skills/information.
- Find an object that does something or will stop something.
- Find a place for a PLOT REASON.
- Slay a demon/monster/villain.
- One of these but not for the reason the MC is told/thinks (plot twist to be revealed at worst possible moment).

Additional main character tropes to think about for fantasy adventures:

- Wishes for adventure/hates adventure.
- Has a lesson to learn.
- Small town and/or small life.
- Has something to prove.
- Unappreciated or worse in current life.
- Has *capacity* for skills, if no actual skills.
- Has surprisingly useful knowledge.

Starting a story with a single scene is a pattern you will follow throughout the genre study weeks. In essays, the unit of construction is the paragraph. **In fiction, the unit of construction is the scene**. Most students think the unit of construction is the chapter, but that is not always the case.

Fantasy scene ideas for getting started:

- Introduce main character – usually a single scene that shows how this person is worthy of the reader's respect, admiration, or at least, interest.

- Introduce the setting – or weave this into the first main character scene.

- Create a problem or a reason the main character has to leave and go do *something*.

- If the problem was caused/is being caused by a Villain, introduce the villain by having them do something *villainous* that's different from the main problem.

From, "Over Normal" by Eva M. 6ᵗʰ Grade

My head pounded as I tugged on my fighting uniform. Class had started a minute ago already, and I was late. I felt like throwing up. Please, please just don't let me have to fight today.

After a minute of leaning against the wall and trying to get the world to stop spinning, someone knocked on the door. Not pounding, just sort of a tapping. I breathed in and took my hand off of the white marble wall.

I opened the door a little and a boy with grayish-purple hair stood there. I recognized him as the boy who was the same dragon species as Isabella, who I saw during the tour. His horns were still spiked like hers, but they were.. purple? I've never seen a Moonthorn dragon with purple horns. Whatever. I just need to hear whatever he had to say and then get out of here.

"Um.. hi," he said nervously, his face flushing. This kid could barely talk. "I-I'm Carson. Mr. Jordan told me to come get you. You're late for class."

I nodded as coldly as possible and walked past him. I probably came off as rude, but that was honestly the least of my issues right now. This kid was probably in with Isabella if he was the same species. Better to have minimal contact with him. The last thing I needed was for him to become a problem.

My stomach dropped as I stepped outside onto the courtyard. The rest of the students were sitting on the bleachers. Two kids were fighting on the mat. One using ice magic and one using light. I felt like I was going to lose the little lunch I ate just looking at them.

Carson rushes up behind me, panting. I ignore him. This kid can't take a hint to save his life. I don't want to talk to you, I think grumpily.

"Mr. Jordan!" he exclaimed. "I got Kate."

A tall man with dark blue hair and gray skin looked over and smiled. "Very good, Carson!" he said happily. "Now we can get on with class."

The two kids fighting on the mat stepped off. The time limit went off, I guess. They returned to the bleachers. I walked over and sat on them as well, Carson following shortly behind me. He sat nowhere near me. Good.

Mr. Jordan (at least, that's what Carson called him) looked at his clipboard and wrote something down. He frowned and glanced at the two students who were fighting on the mat. I guess they didn't do so well.

He kept glancing from his clipboard to us, occasionally making a note. After about a minute, he put his pen down.

"My next two students who will be fighting are."

Please not me. Please, please please please please please don't pick me.

"Kate and Carson."

NO!

My stomach dropped to the floor. I recovered quickly and tried to put on my best 'eh, okay' face, but my stomach was swirling like I had eaten the meatloaf they served in middle school. A few kids started whispering behind me.

"Hey, Carson's finally up. He's a Moonthorn psychic, right? And look what Lola did to Finn; if that's a weak psychic, Carson could absolutely annihilate this girl!"

If being picked wasn't bad enough, this comment made me almost lose my lunch for the second time in ten minutes. Now this purple-haired boy who was nothing but a nuisance two minutes ago is now going to beat the living snot out of me?

I hate this school.

Table 3.1 Mentor Texts Fantasy

Fantasy	Type of Book	Title	Author
	Picture book	Sukey and the Mermaid	Robert San Souci
	Picture book	The Paperbag Princess	Robert Munsch
	Early reader	Zoey and Sassafras: Dragons and Marshmallows	Asia Citro
	Early reader	Unicorn Academy	Julie Sykes
	Middle grade	Where the Mountain Meets the Moon	Grace Lin
	Middle grade	Tristan Strong Punches a Hole in the Sky	Kwame Mbalia
	Middle grade	The Storm Runner	J.C. Cervantes
	Middle grade	Warriors	Erin Hunter
	Middle grade	Wings of Fire	Tui T. Sutherland
	Young adult	Ember in the Ashes	Sabaa Tahir
	Young adult	Wicked Fox	Kat Cho
	Young adult	We Set the Dark on Fire	Taylor Kay Mejia

Lesson Ideas – Crime Fiction

If you want your students' undivided attention, opening the class by announcing, "Today we'll begin our study of crime," usually does the trick. Crime fiction permeates popular culture, especially television, but it predates television, film, and games with its written tradition. More than half of your students have heard of Agatha Christie, and another quarter will have heard of the relatively recent reboot of *Murder on the Orient Express* and *Death on the Nile* films. (Branagh, Kenneth, director. Twentieth Century Fox, 2017.)

Crime – Day 1 – Overview and Mystery

* Advance prep – BEFORE you begin Crime week, search headlines for words that connect to Mystery, Suspense, or Thriller.

- A robbery headline can be linked to mystery (stolen jewelry or stolen art).
- A suspense headline should be about an ongoing investigation of a series of crimes (robberies, murders, kidnappings).
- A thriller headline will be about "Police/FBI/Interpol race(s) to stop X happening before X event."

Warm-Up and Overview

Post the three headlines and the accompanying photos (use your best judgment, of course). The writing prompt is: *Which of these is mystery, which is suspense, and which is thriller? Choose the one that interests you the most to write a little more about.*

Once everyone's written a bit, including you, use Figure 3.1 to show students the answers. This three-column chart if helpful because it shows the similarities and differences across these three sub-genres of crime fiction.

In a mystery, the crime happens in chapter one or before the story starts. The crime is ongoing in suspense stories. And in thrillers, the challenge is to stop the crime before it happens. Are there exceptions to these ideas? Absolutely. But this is an excellent place to start when deciding what sort of crime fiction to try.

3 Genres Much Like Each Other

Mystery	Suspense	Thriller
(already happened)	(is happening now)	(is about to happen)
• Crime: Murder, Robbery, etc.	• Crime: kidnapping, murder(s), robbery, etc.	• Plot: bomb, kidnapping, attack,
• Clues/False Clues	• Suspects	• Ticking clock
• Suspects	• Clues	• High stakes - large scale impact
• Detective (professional or amateur)	• High stakes	• Law enforcement professional - FBI, CIA, etc.
• Has to be solved	• Law enforcement professional - police, etc.	• Stopped
	• Solved or stopped	

Figure 3.1 Mystery, suspense, and thriller

Crime fiction has been called "The Language of Justice" and it is the most commonly published type of genre fiction, after Romance. Crime fiction provides a sense of closure and satisfaction because the crime is solved or stopped, and the villain is caught and/or punished. Crime fiction also interests readers and writers who love puzzles and love to feel smart or successful as they read.

In mystery – the crime and the location of the crime must match the detective/protagonist.

For example, if someone has stolen the brand-new climbing wall on the day it was supposed to be installed in the school gym, the protagonist of this story could be a student or a teacher.

Cozy mysteries are a sub-genre of Mystery that feature an amateur sleuth with a completely different day job than solving crime. Readers of cozy mysteries love protagonists with hobbies or occupations like chef, crossword puzzle expert, dog groomer, ballroom dancer, etc. These hobbies and occupations give the protagonist a special set of skills that help with the mysteries set, for example, at catered events on Cape Cod.

One of my favorite middle grade mysteries is Half Moon Investigations by Eoin Colfer (author of the Artemis Fowl novels). This would be an excellent mentor text for 4th and 5th grade students writing mysteries. The protagonist is a child who manages to get in and out of believable trouble as he attempts to solve a crime for a student at his school. (Colfer, Eoin. Miramax Books, 2006.) For additional mentor text ideas for crime fiction, refer to Table 3.2 at the end of this section.

The last piece of overview information is the evidence triangle used by law enforcement: Means, Motive, and Opportunity. In order for a perpetrator to be convicted of a crime, it must be proven that the individual had the means (the poison, the weapon, etc.) to commit the crime, the motive, as in a reason to commit the crime, and the opportunity, meaning the perpetrator was available and unaccounted for during the window in which the crime was committed. Also, take a brief moment to define "alibi."

 ## *Mini-Lesson*

1. Choose your protagonist/detective.
   a. Decide if this person is a generalized amateur sleuth, like Nancy Drew or a specialized amateur sleuth with a specific skill set, as mentioned above. The other option for mystery is a private detective protagonist, like Hercule Poirot, from several Agatha Christie novels or Sherlock Holmes. This type of protagonist has significantly above average skills in observation and logic.
2. Choose the crime (robbery or a single murder – keep it within PG and PG-13 boundaries).
3. Choose the location of the crime (this has to match the protagonist and the type of crime).
4. List legit and false clues.
5. List legit and false suspects.

These are all brainstorms in the writer's notebook, nothing formal, just getting the ingredients together before you start cooking. These things may/ will change as the writing goes along. For students who aren't sure how to start, this type of jotting will feel very productive.

Once everyone has a few ideas for each of the five steps, they're ready to try a scene. Some ideas to try:

- Discovering the crime scene – either a main character, a minor character, or a possible suspect could do this, clues should be hidden and/ or visible.

- The main character fails at the first attempted solution – is this done in public? Or is the main character alone when this happens? What might cause this person to fail? Arrogance? Impatience? Were they tricked?

- An important clue is discovered by the protagonist – this could be the clue that finally gets the investigator on the right track, the clue could be to how the crime was committed or who committed the crime.

Other scenes to try from the vast list of mystery tropes:

Blood-Stained Letter, Did Not Die That Way, Intrepid Reporter, Locked Room Mystery, Motive Equals Conclusive Evidence, Not-So-Fake Prop Weapon, Absence of Evidence, Beneath Suspicion, The Butler Did It, Eagle Eye Detection, Evidence Scavenger Hunt, Finger Licking Poison, Hidden in Plain Sight, Stakeout, You Meddling Kids, etc.

Crime Day 2 – Suspense

Warm-Up

For today's writing opener choose images of things like:

- Children on a playground
- A crowded airport
- An abandoned or wrecked car
- The emergency entrance to a hospital

The writing prompt is: *Choose one of these images and use it to describe something your main character might be worried about.*

Once everyone has had some time to write and to share a word or a sentence with a colleague, bring the group back together and put the word SUSPENSE on the screen or the board.

Explain that suspense is a *technique* used by all fiction writers, across all genres, to keep the reader turning the page. Usually, suspense is created by a lingering worry the main character has, such as Will, wondering if he has the courage to avenge his brother's murder, in *Long Way Down* by Jason Reynolds (Simon and Schuster, 2017).

 ## Mini-Lesson

For today's purposes, we're working on Suspense as a sub-genre of Crime Fiction. Generally, suspense novels are about danger or the threat of ongoing danger. That being said, the danger is relative to the main character's situation, skills, and environment.

Suspense falls between Mysteries and Thrillers in terms of pacing. Suspense stories tend to move faster or have a shorter timeline than Mysteries but might move slower or have a longer timeline than a traditional Thriller.

Go back to the three-column graphic and look at how Suspense compares across the other indicators, like types of characters. Highlight that in Suspense, the writer can add a villain point of view. Quite often the main character knows who the villain is and also what the current and potential future crimes might be – the trick is to stop the villain before they can continue their villainy.

The following are the steps to writing a suspense novel:

1. Determine the stakes – this is a good time to remind students about your PG or PG-13 boundaries.
   a. Usually life or death.
   b. If not actual life or death, must be as extreme as life or death to Main Character.
2. Determine how many point of view (PoV) characters will "tell" the story – this is a great opportunity to try third-person omniscient and add multiple PoV's.
3. Spend time developing a sympathetic, relatable protagonist – so readers will care what happens to them.
4. Create obstacles for the main character, big and small, personal and professional.

Some students will be ready to write using these steps, some will want to break down each step and mull it over with you or a partner. Use mentor texts to investigate how authors make these steps their own.

Suspense scenes to try:

- Establishment of the villain – have the villain do something that shows how terrible they are.
- The main character finds a much worse crime scene and realizes how much more complicated/terrible the problem is.
- Something "small" in the main character's life derails their actions on the main problem.
- Someone important in the main character's life is suddenly involved in the main problem.

Suspense Tropes that could become scenes: Lights Off – Somebody Dies, Ripped from the Headlines, Anonymous Killer Narrator, Consulting a Convicted Criminal, Evil Plan, Spot the Imposter

Crime Day 3 – Thriller

Thriller is the fastest paced of these three types of Crime fiction. Thrillers tend to have the highest stakes, the largest potential crimes, and therefore require some sort of professional as a main character. For students who did not connect with Fantasy tropes, Crime is usually where understanding kicks in. You will see a lot of "ah-ha" moments in your students by the end of this week.

Warm-Up

Today's writing warm-up is about action, a key component of the Thriller subgenre. Using age-appropriate images (including from cartoons) invite students to write or draw/write one of these action sequences.

- A rescue from a building on fire.
- A fight on the roof of a high-rise.

- A car chase through the downtown of (your city or the nearest big city).
- And the classic – defusing a bomb.

Before the short sharing routine, ask the students to add an element to the action that would create more challenge for the person attempting to solve the problem. If they're not sure, they might try innocent bystanders at risk, a sudden and severe change in the weather (trying to defuse a bomb in a hurricane!), or a phone call from the person's mom. [There's a funny Geico commercial where this happens. You might want to show it. All their commercials are archived on their YouTube channel https://www.youtube.com/user/GEICO.]

Mini-Lesson

Go back to the three-column chart and quickly review the elements of Thrillers. Then show a movie trailer from this genre. I'm partial to the Hobbs & Shaw trailer (*Leitch, David, director. Universal Pictures, 2019*) and ask students to talk through the tropes out loud.

Plot: A virus that "melts your cells" will be unleashed on the world.
Ticking clock: "in 72 hours."
High Stakes: "the virus will wipe out nearly half of the world's population."
Personal Stakes: For Hobbs – his daughter; For Shaw – his mother and sister
Law enforcement characters: CIA (special group).
A truly great villain: In this case a genetically altered super soldier working for a high-tech shadow organization.
Other Thriller tropes this trailer highlights: Multiple types of action including physical fights, car chases, explosions, and travel to exotic locations. And, a special fun trope called "People who hate each other having to work together" with a touch of "I think your sister's cute" thrown in as well.

Many film franchises, with mostly PG-13 ratings, showcase the thriller genre. James Bond is always an option, as are the *Mission Impossible* films.

To do this warm-up with younger students, I would use *Spies in Disguise* or potentially the old *Kim Possible* cartoons from the Disney channel.

Campbell, Martin, director. Casino Royale. Metro-Goldwyn-Mayer Pictures/ Sony Pictures, 2006.

Cruise, Tom, et al. Mission: Impossible– Ghost Protocol. Paramount Pictures, 2011.

Quane, Troy and Nick Bruno, directors. Spies in Disguise. Blue Sky Studios/ Twentieth Century Fox, 2019.

Schooley, Bob, et al. Kim Possible, episode Season 1 Trailer, 2002.

Recipe for a Thriller

1. Choose the main character: Do they work for an organization? What special skills, tools, tech might they have? Does the main character have a team?
2. Choose the problem to be prevented.
3. How much time on the clock? (Shouldn't be longer than a week.)
4. What are the stakes nationally or globally?
5. What are the personal stakes for the main character?
6. List locations where main events will take place.
7. List successes and failures: (the main character cannot succeed on the first try – readers like to see a powerful, skilled protagonist fail, and then overcome that failure).

Just as with suspense, some students will want to work through this recipe independently, some will want support from you or a peer.

Scenes to try:

- Establish the skills/team/organization of the main character by introducing them in the middle or near the end of solving a problem that is not the problem of the new story (but the two problems could be linked if you're feeling fancy).
- A non-field operative, like the science advisor, explains and demonstrates the consequences of the thing the main character is trying to stop.

- The team experiences a major setback.
- Personal stakes distract or derail the main character from the mission.

Thriller tropes that could become scenes: the main character is literally hanging from a cliff or a tall building, this is all a conspiracy, someone on the inside betrayed us, more than one bomb, the main character is tortured by a memory and/or atoning for something, weapons of opportunity/anything can be a weapon

Crime Fiction Bonus Section – Villains!

While we need villains in many types of fiction, Crime Fiction is made stronger and more compelling through its villains. A case could be made that every Sherlock needs a Moriarty. To support students choosing to add a Villain PoV character or for fun, add a mini-lesson about Villains to your study of Crime Fiction. (Doyle, Arthur Conan. "The Adventure of the Final Problem." The Memoirs of Sherlock Holmes, Strand Magazine, 1893.)

Villains should not be confused with Anti-Heroes although they share some of the same qualities. For example, Gru in *Despicable Me* is a reformed villain who now (albeit reluctantly) does mostly good deeds. Therefore, he is no longer "the villain" in the story. Han Solo, from the *Star Wars* franchise, is a criminal, specifically a smuggler, when viewers first meet him. Just like Gru, Han Solo mostly turns his skills to support the forces of good. Reformed criminals make great main characters in crime fiction because they have the ability to assess a situation from the criminal's point of view, aka, they have insider knowledge on how to steal a valuable painting or kidnap an heiress. Before you dive into villains you might do a "Villain or Anti-Hero?" set of images to practice this somewhat tricky concept.

Meledandri, Chris, et al. Despicable Me. Universal, 2010.

Lucas, George. Star Wars (Franchise). Lucasfilm Ltd./Twentieth Century Fox, 1977.

Coogler, Ryan, director. Black Panther. Marvel Studios/Walt Disney Studios, 2018.

Next choose a Villain you/your students know well from recent books or films. I like to use Eric Killmonger, from the first *Black Panther* film. Then I show the following checklist (adapted from http://www.jerryjenkins.com/ makes-great-villain-checklist-writing-good-bad-guy/) and talk through how Killmonger exhibits many of these traits.

- They have many likable qualities.
- They're convinced they are the hero!
- They are a worthy enough/skilled enough opponent to make your hero look good.
- You (and your reader) like when they're on stage.
- They are clever and accomplished enough that people must lend them begrudging respect.
- They can't be a fool or a bumbler.
- They have many of the same characteristics of the hero, but they're misdirected.
- They should occasionally be kind and not just for show.
- They can be merciless, even to the innocent.
- They are persuasive.
- They will stop at nothing to get what they want.
- They are proud.
- They are deceitful.
- They are vengeful.
- They are jealous, especially of the hero.

As we're enjoying thinking about villainous villains, we should be sure to use at least a few female villains as examples. Even though the phrase "bad guy" feels so common as to be universal, it's still gendered. Disney gives us a few examples like Ursula and Cruella Deville. *Divergent* by Veronica Roth (Katherin Teegan books, 2011) also has a female villain.

From, "DEXTER AND LYN" by Naomi K.

"Dexter! Where are you?" I started panicking. Where was he? "Dexter!" I leaned against a tree. How was I supposed to find him? It's not like these woods are small. I decided I should rest, and keep looking for him when I was ready. But something kept telling me to stay awake and alert, that something was out there and I should keep my guard up. It wasn't easy staying away, and after a while my eyelids began to feel like weights and it was a struggle to keep them open. I would slip in and out of consciousness, and would scold myself when I was out. It wasn't until a sharp shriek sliced the air that I shot up. I was flooded with a wave of tasks in my mind, but I pushed them out of my head. I needed to find Dexter. And I needed to figure out what that sound was.

"Lyn!" I've been searching for at least an hour already. Where is she? She must be searching for me too, but where? I pause for a moment to take in my surroundings. Trees. Darkness. Shadows. How do I survive here? How do I find Lyn? I slip out of my backpack and check my supplies again. Water, sunscreen, trail mix, a whistle, a watch, a blanket, and some bug spray. Why did I not bring my compass? I wondered if Lyn still had her backpack, or if she left it behind after the attack. If she did, she could survive for a little. If she didn't, then I would have to find her before she starves. Or freezes. The odds are not in my favor.

I should've had my backpack. I wonder if Dexter has his. I hope so. I hope he wasn't as stupid as I was in leaving my backpack when we got attacked. I angered myself just thinking about it. It was all my fault. I should've thought ahead. He's probably worrying about me, and me dying. And I probably will. I'll make him suffer. Unless I find him. I stood up, and stretched. I began to pack up, but realized that I don't have anything except for a water bottle and a sweatshirt. I start jogging through the woods, hoping for a sound, sight, or even scent that tells me I'm looking in the right direction. I keep up the pace, now running steadily over the pine needles. I stop after about an hour to drink some water and rest. I find a good spot and settle down. I wrap myself in my sweatshirt and close my eyes. Just rest… I thought. I did not want to sleep. Just rest…

I kept shouting for her. I would not stop. Ever. I would not stop protecting her. No matter what she does to me. "Lyn?" I turned around. I had been walking this way for already two hours. I started running, using all the energy I had to run the way that I had been walking for hours. I felt like I wasn't doing anything productive, so I grabbed my water bottle and sat down. I began to take little sips, careful to not spill any. I layed out my priorities:

5. Find Lyn (or her backpack)
6. Find Lyn
7. Find a river and refill water.
8. Find our way back home. Without getting killed.

A lot of finding stuff. I don't know if I have that much time. Maybe it'll be easier if I find my sister. If not, I might as well die. I sat up straight. I heard a faint "Dexter" but it was too far away to hear where it was coming from. "Lyn!" I yelled, but someone beat me to it. Someone else was out there. And they were trying to get to my sister.

Table 3.2 Mentor Texts Crime

Crime	Type of Book	Title	Author
	Picture book	Miss Nelson is Missing!	James Marshall
*Humor	Early reader	The Bad Guys	Aaron Blabey
	Early reader	InvestiGators	John Patrick Green
	Early reader	Nate the Great	Marjorie Weinman Sharmat
	Middle grade	Me, Frida, and the Secret of the Peacock Ring	Angela Cervantes
*Humor	Middle grade	Half Moon Investigations	Eoin Colfer
	Middle grade	Spy School	Stuart Gibbs
*Historical	Middle grade	The Westing Game	Ellen Raskin
	Middle grade	H.I.V.E.	Mark Walden
	Middle grade	Theodore Boone: Kid Lawyer	John Grisham
	Middle grade/ young adult	Stormbreaker (Alex Rider series)	Anthony Horowitz
	Young adult	The Inheritance Games	Jennifer Lynn Barnes
	Young adult	I Hunt Killers	Barry Lyga
	Young adult	One of Us is Lying	E. Lockhart

Lesson Ideas – Science Fiction

Some people love Science Fiction for the big open universe of unexplored ideas it offers. And some people dislike Science Fiction for this exact reason – it's too much, too unstructured, too "out there." Science Fiction is informed by what we know *now*. Compare five minutes of the 1982 film *Tron* with five minutes from the 2010 film *Tron: Legacy*. What humanity understood about games and game technology in 1982 limited the imagination of the filmmakers. (Depending on when you're reading this book, the game tech from 2010 will look out of date as well, but slightly *less* out of date.) And yet, some writers pushed beyond these limits and stretched their ideas far beyond what was yet to be imagined. And in doing so, pushed readers' imaginations as well. For some of your students, the open *possibility* in science fiction will be the perfect invitation to write.

Lisberger, Steven. Tron. Buena Vista Pictures, 1982.

Kosinsky, Joseph, director. Tron: Legacy. Walt Disney Pictures, 2010.

Science Fiction Day 1 – Overview and Characters

Science fiction is a genre of speculative fiction typically dealing with imaginative concepts such as futuristic science and technology, space travel, time travel, faster than light travel, parallel universes, and extraterrestrial life.

As Ray Bradbury says, "In Science Fiction, we dream."

Warm-Up

Use an image for each of these prompts:

- Time Travel – Explain to your history professor why you need access to the school's time machine in order to study_____.
- Space Flight – Your parents are scientists and you were born on a deep space research vessel. For your 15th birthday, they're taking you home to Earth. Describe how you feel and what you see when you arrive.

- Parallel Universe – A version of yourself from a parallel universe is taking over your life. How are you similar and different from this person, meaning, how can loved ones tell you apart? What can you learn from your "counterpart"? Why have they come to your universe?
- Future Tech – "Why grieve when you can preserve the dearly departed in Perma-Glass?"

After students have shared out from their warm-up writing, show the short three-minute video, "Fiction Book Genres - What is Science Fiction?" from Molding Minds (Sept. 2014, moldingminds.com/video-fiction-genres-science-fiction). This is funny, informative, and uses Legos to illustrate the various aspects of Science Fiction, including how SF is different from Fantasy.

Use a simple slide with an image from a popular game. I use a screen cap from the Fallout series (Interplay Productions, 1997) to reinforce the following key elements of Science Fiction:

- Must be Set in the Future (or in a version of the past, or now that is perceptibly different from reality).
- Must have Science!
- Usually Asks a big "What if" question.

Brainstorm Mentor Texts

Just like during the Fantasy overview, post a few images of current television shows, games, books, and films that are categorized as Science Fiction. Give students 90 seconds to get as many of their own mentor texts written in their notebooks. Be ready to ask, "is the central problem caused by Science?" if students name something unfamiliar. If zombies and superheroes didn't come up during your Fantasy conversation, now is a good time to clarify that 99% of the time, zombie problems in fiction are/ were caused by science. Only about 1% of the time in fiction are zombies created through magic. Most superheroes/supervillains' powers are also created by science. However, some are created by magic – Black Panther, Wonder Woman, and Thor are examples of this. A list of mentor texts for Science Fiction can be found in Table 3.3 at the end of this section.

Mini-Lesson

Just as with Fantasy and Crime Fiction, readers won't stick with a Science Fiction story if they can't connect with the characters. Some of the early, pioneering greats in Sci Fi, like Octavia Butler and Isaac Asimov, used accessible, relatable characters to draw readers into radically new futures and possibilities for humankind.

Hopefully, by now, students are seeing the pattern that *most types of genre fiction start with character work*. If not, you might want to point out the pattern.

Characters in Science Fiction

For this slide I use an image from the film *Rogue One* (Edwards, Gareth, director. Walt Disney Studios, 2016.)

- Robots
- Aliens
- Cyborgs
- Computers
- Zombies
- Mutants
- Superheroes
- Clones
- Humans

Ask students to consider what or who might be missing from this list. Next ask them to work with a partner or small group to come up with examples (game, film, television, book) of each of these types of characters. Some of your students will want to divide aliens and superheroes into sub-categories. They might also want to tag groups or types of characters more likely to be protagonists, more likely to be sidekicks, more likely to be villains, etc. Some of your students will want and maybe *need* to draw characters at this point, which is great.

Next, ask students to pick a character to write a little more about. I use a tiny piece I wrote from the perspective of Dr. Bruce Banner, aka The Hulk, as my example. (And yes, this is fan fiction that we'll dig into later.)

If they're not sure where to start, ask students to pick a problem for the character and write about that. Their list of character examples should help them here. For example, one problem for Chewbacca is that not very many humans speak Wookie. A problem for a computer might be that it can't move itself around without help. Cyborg's human parts might be less reliable and more vulnerable than their machine parts.

Thinking homework: Science Fiction Day 2 will be about setting, so assign students the homework of *thinking about* possible settings for a science fiction story. They might want to invite caregivers and/or siblings into a conversation as part of the homework.

Remember that one of the writerly activities on the anchor chart is thinking and/or daydreaming. Assigning thinking for homework instead of writing for homework, reinforces this notion and is completely authentic to the professional writer experience. I can't count the number of times I've been distracted by my own thoughts as a new exciting story idea took shape.

Science Fiction Day 2 – Setting

I've had great luck with searches like, "city of the future" "alien planet" "Mars colony" etc. Pick one to use for the first prompt which is to Download Your Thinking Homework. Not every student will have remembered to do their thinking homework, so this gives them some thinking time. But others will have had robust thoughts and/or conversations at home and have lots to download into their notebooks.

After students have been writing (and you too, of course) for about five minutes, get everyone together and see if you can collect some idea trends. If you're so inclined, this is a moment to change up the sharing protocols you've been using since students are sharing out *ideas* and not necessarily writing. I like "walk around until the music stops and find a partner" for idea sharing sometimes. Anything to get in a little movement since writing is, by necessity, sedentary.

Mini-Lesson

If you search things like "Star Trek Schematic," you will get cool diagrams of the starships. Show one of these and ask students if creating a setting for a science fiction story might require drawing a map.

Ask, is a schematic a kind of map? (The answer is yes, of course. If one were writing a story about space pirates, the locations of the cargo hold and the bridge of the ship being pirated would be critical to the story.) If you wanted to use a film clip here to illustrate the importance of locations and spaces on a star ship, you could use one from the Axiom, the ship from *WALL-E* (Stanton, Andrew, et al. Walt Disney Studios Motion Pictures, 2008), or the famous trash compacter scene from *Star Wars* episode IV (Lucas, George. Star Wars (Franchise). Lucasfilm Ltd./ Twentieth Century Fox, 1977).

Unlike Fantasy, which is almost always one planet, one continent, or even one town, Science Fiction novels might span multiple galaxies. Maps can be important to show what resources are where, who has military bases, shortest, riskiest means to travel from point A to point B, and many more reasons.

Show a list of common settings in Science Fiction (along with a cool picture). Invite students to add common settings that might be missing.

- Another planet
- Future Earth
- An alien city/planet
- Spaceship/Starship
- Alternate dimension
- Space colony
- The Moon

Technology

Settings in Science Fiction generally include lots of technology. Sometimes the technology is mysterious but working and sometimes it doesn't work. The Netflix reboot of *She-Ra and the Princesses of Power* has some great examples of humans discovering "ancient alien tech" that only sort of works. (Stephenson, Noelle. She-Ra and the Princesses of Power, Season 1, Netflix, Nov. 2018.)

If your students want to borrow tech from existing Science Fiction storylines, such as warp speed or teleporting, let them. If they invent new tech, ask them to explain a little about how the science of that tech works or at least to make up a story about how the tech was discovered. The mentor texts will have examples of how authors do this. For example, you could show the scene where Doc explains to Marty how he invented the flux capacitor in *Back to the Future* (Zemeckis, Robert, director. Universal Pictures/Amblin Entertainment, 1985). Or, you could show one of several scenes from Shuri's lab in *Black Panther* (Coogler, Ryan, director. Marvel Studios/Walt Disney Studios, 2018) when she's explaining to her brother how one of her inventions works. Readers love near-future tech and completely mysterious tech. Some students will fall right down the bleeding edge tech wormhole at this point. Let them. That research might turn into high-interest technical writing, instead of Science Fiction, and that's great.

The last part of the Science Fiction setting work is to choose a setting that might fit the character they wrote about yesterday or choose a new setting and write about it. They might need to sketch a bit here as well. As students write, they're mining for how characters connect to or reflect the setting and also looking for obvious and hidden problems within the setting. Do emphasize the idea of setting and character problems because that's where we start tomorrow, with story problems.

Science Fiction Day 3 – Plot Tropes

When I'm talking with students about Science Fiction plot tropes, I find myself saying things like, "Who doesn't love a good alien invasion, am I right?" But one of the secrets of Science Fiction, even more than Fantasy, is the stories are always about something else. You might start off writing a story about an alien invasion, but the plot ends up revealing how a small group of humans might respond under stress and fear. This is the plot of the Twilight Zone classic episode, "The Monsters are Due on Maple Street" (Serling, Rod. *The Twilight Zone*. Season 1, Mar. 1960.).

Warm-Up

Put 2–3 headlines on the screen of current and/or upcoming science innovations and ask, "What surprise discoveries might emerge? What could go wrong?" Be sure to include one headline that doesn't have to do with space. Lots of interesting things are happening with ocean exploration for example, as well as scientific research in Antarctica. Did you know a library of killer bacteria exists? I mean, what could go wrong? Even though Science Fiction isn't as regularly taken from headlines as Crime Fiction is, the science articles from major news organizations *always* have interesting story ideas to borrow.

After everyone has written and the class has had a chance to share out, ask everyone to look at the setting and character problems they jotted down at the end of class on Day 2. Invite them to add a few more problem ideas.

Mini-Lesson

Show this list of Science Fiction Plot Tropes:

- Exploration
- Dystopia/Utopia (might be related to post-apocalyptic scenarios)
- Alien invasion (friendly or hostile)
- Time travel
- Genetic engineering
- Dimensional travel
- Computer virus or EMP (electro-magnetic pulse)
- Zombie apocalypse
- Mutants helping/taking over

Once you've made sure everyone understands the basics of these common Science Fiction plot tropes, invite students to revisit their mentor text lists and see if they can match any of these plot tropes with the titles they jotted down. As they're working, they might think of additional ideas for mentor texts.

A related thought: some YA and MG science fiction novels are adventure-based plots, essentially an adventure story that happens to take place in space. *The Disasters* by M.K England (HarperTeen, an Imprint of Harper Collins Publishers, 2019) is a good example along with the *Aurora*

Cycle books by Amie Kaufman and Jay Kristoff (Knopf Books for Young Readers, 2019). Those have more of the adventure/quest-type plot tropes, with space and technology as essential components of the story.

Put it all together and make notes about the three key elements of story: Character, Setting, and Plot. Even if students aren't sure this is the genre they want to write, invite them to note/draw the elements they like best in these categories and what they would include if assigned to write Science Fiction.

Give students plenty of time to write today, at least 20 minutes. As part of this writing time, they might note questions that have come up, patterns they've noticed about themselves as writers or the genres studied so far, and mentor texts they're interested in reading/viewing/playing.

From "Alex and Evan's Story" by N. Murphy, 7th Grade

Adam raised his hands to his temples and very aggressively squinted at me.

"What are you doing?" I asked in a very concerned voice.

"Trying to remember something, maybe, maybe not." He spoke those words with more difficulty than was needed, probably because he was busy wasting brain cells over nothing.

"Are you done?" I asked.

"Not yet… and… now I am."

He gave me an impish smile and went over to his holo message. He stared at it until the clock turned to 3:00 which was a very awkward seven minutes for me because I didn't know what to do while he was intensely staring, once the clock turned to three he turned to me and said: "Hey, look it's thre-" but he was cut off in the middle of his sentence by the sound of gears turning from somewhere underneath us.

There was a three-second period of silence until a loud POP broke the silence in the room or box or whatever you would call it, the holo messages shut off and a pedestal rose from the center of the room where a small cube with nine colored squares on each side rested on top. I was about to be confused for the eightieth time within the last 20 minutes when Adam yelled, "It's a Rubix Cube!! I love these things! I think! I have no clue but I'm going to do it anyway!"

He raced towards the pedestal and grabbed the cube. A few moments after he removed it from its pedestal, a loud noise rang through the room, and a few small sections of the floor opened up and retreated further into the floor, and a thick red fog started to pour out of them.

"Really? You had to grab it off of an obvious trap."

"Yes, I did."

He closed his eyes and stuck his tongue out at me, and I felt like I was about to hit him when a holo message square dropped from the ceiling and hit him on the top of the head, "Ow!"

I picked it up and turned it on as I did with the previous one. The recording activated and read the message, "Looks like you activated the puzzle, good thing it was sooner rather than later. To escape this room you must solve the Rubix cube before the acid gas can get into your lungs. Don't worry about your skin; it won't be affected."

Adam began to furiously turn the sides of the Rubix Cube; with each twist of the cube, his eyes got brighter in color until they were like electric storms and at one point I could swear he looked like he was sparking. I stared at him and at how fast he turned the corners in a repeating pattern over and over until with a click, the cube was complete. He looked up at me with that same impish grin from earlier and said, "I told you I love Rubix Cubes. Maybe." He placed the cube back on the pedestal, and with a click, the pedestal retreated into the floor. The walls separated into a large corridor.

I opened my mouth to speak, but the words didn't come out until my third try, "I guess we go through there?" My mind rushed around trying to figure out why it happened so fast, That was too easy. There has to be something else. Adam began to walk down the corridor with a proud smile hanging on his face and turned to me, "Hurry up, Alexand... Nah, I don't like that. How about Alex instead? It is shorter and easier to say." "I think you're right, it's too long." I ran and caught up with him.

"How did you know how to solve the Cube?"

"I don't know, muscle memory, I guess, maybe?"

"Well, we should get out of here before something else happe..." a sliding sound and a loud hiss from behind us indicated that I had jinxed myself, I turned around. I saw that the floor had opened up even more than before and even opened in new places, and a red fog poured out at alarmingly fast speeds. More sections of the ground opened every second, and parts of the wall lowered just as fast. "I just had to open my mouth!"

From about twenty feet in front of us, a creature crawled out of the floor. Its fur was dark as night, and it had claws the same length of a human hand, it's body was vaguely humanoid but its head was that of a human's. It bared its teeth and inclined its wolf-like head to look me in its pale silver eyes.

I turned to Adam, "Run?"

"Agreed!"

Table 3.3 Mentor Texts Science Fiction

Science Fiction	Type of Book	Title	Author
	Picture book	The Three Little Aliens and the Big Bad Robot	Margaret McNamara
*Humor	Early reader	EngiNerds	Jarrett Learner
	Middle grade	The Maze Runner	James Dashner
	Middle grade	The Wild Robot	Peter Brown
	Middle grade	Sal and Gabi Break the Universe	Carlos Hernandez
	Young adult	Scythe	Neal Shusterman
	Young adult	Illuminae	Amie Kaufman and Jay Kristoff
	Young adult	Ship Breaker	Paolo Bacigalupi
	Young adult	Superman: Dawnbreaker	Matt de la Peña

Ask Your Students

Some of your students will have heard the old saying, "Write what you know." Writing what you know is great practice. BUT, I love the updated version of the question, especially for genre fiction which is, "Write what you WANT TO KNOW." I've started to use this interchangeably with my overarching guideline, "Write what you want to read."

A great way to kick off these next few weeks of genre fiction is to ask, "What do you need to know in order to write what you want to read?"

This is a super hard question.

You will get responses like, "how to start" and "how to get ideas for a story" and from the kids looking toward the horizon, "how does a book get published." Another question which helps me figure out mentor text matches for students is, "Who/What do you want to write like?" To clarify this, you might point out reviews which often say, "For fans of X. Or if you liked Y, you will love Z."

Depending on your comfort in your role as teacher-writer, you might have examples of your own to share, for example, you might want to write like Walter Dean Meyers or Gary Soto. I often share that I admire two horror writers, Jonathan Stroud who writes for the middle-grade audience, and Jonathan Maberry, who writes both YA and adult horror. What I admire is the amount of heart the characters have, and how both writers put as much care into the characters as they do into the tension and the plot elements. And how, in a genre that often gets the side-eyes from proponents of literary fiction, their use of figurative language is unique and beautiful.

Usually, when I share that I like horror, and explain that I was trying to write a creepy ghost story and needed to study what these two authors did that made their books so chilling, it elicits another round of questions like, "how to make people scared" and "how to make a story funny" and "how to make people feel like they're falling into the world of your story."

Knowing that this whole section is about the genres the class wanted to learn, you get to have that special *I'm a Magician* feeling that teachers enjoy on the best days. You get to collect all their questions and say, "Yes, we're going to learn all these things as we write together. Are you ready to try?"

By the end of Crime Fiction, student writing behavior has usually started to shift. I often find myself holding my breath at first because I'm waiting for the group to settle and for the community trust to build. But it always does. Honestly, that shift, above all other reasons, is why I wanted to write this book. The miracle of watching students *choose* to write is one I wanted you to experience in your classrooms. It's too wonderful not to share.

Savvy teachers know it's important to catch students doing something great, but also to not make a huge deal out of it. Instead share a few things you've noticed by the end of week 3 or week 5, like, "I noticed most of you get working in your writers' notebooks more quickly." Or, "I noticed different people sharing parts of their writing this week." Or, "I noticed some of you are writing a lot of words." Then you might also talk about what you've noticed in yourself, such as, "At first I was a little nervous to try Crime Fiction, but I'm really enjoying writing fight scenes." Or, "I used to worry about writing time and if it was working. But now it's my favorite part of the day."

Ask Yourself

Think back on the writing instruction you received as a K-12 student. Did you have the opportunity to write across multiple genres and purposes for writing? And in which of those did you receive direct instruction? Beginning in 9th grade, I received excellent instruction in the art of the five-paragraph essay. And I'm grateful for that education. Back then, and even now, the ability to write a tight five-paragraph essay is the key to many doors. Prior to high school, I wrote reports and the occasional "creative" story with my spelling words, but I don't recall actual instruction for either of those. We probably received a checklist of things to include…and an admonishment not to plagiarize.

Fast forward to your teacher training. Did you have a class called, "How to teach writing"? If so, wonderful! You're one of the lucky few. I ask teachers this question everywhere I go and most often answers are about a "Secondary Literacy" class or "Middle Grade Literature" or "Balanced Literacy." I don't ask, "Did you have a class called How to Teach Gifted Writers?" I already know the answer.

Writing is supposed to be included in the umbrella of Literacy, but very often the only writing we learn how to teach is *in response to reading*.

Think about the incredibly structured methods for teaching persuasive and informational writing. 99% of the time those structures are linked to a text or texts the individual or the group just read. Okay, now think about your comfort level using those methods. Depending on how long you've been teaching, you probably have a solid repertoire of exemplars, mentor texts, and trouble-shooting tricks. You've probably learned how to diagnose common persuasive and informational writing challenges and have a handful of remedies that usually work. Do you have strategies to stretch your gifted informational and persuasive writers? You might give them a more complex text or text set to incorporate into their essay. But to grow their technique? If the rubric you use doesn't point the way toward growth, it's hard to know what to do except give a pat on the back and move on.

Informational and persuasive writing becomes richer and more compelling through the use of narrative tools. Teaching these things directly shines a light where your strongest writers have been fumbling in the dark. The bonus of teaching genres and narrative tools is that your students finally see a direct connection between what you're doing in writer's workshop and the most obvious writing product in a school: Books. And that's what your struggling and reluctant writers need, a sense of purpose and why doing this writing stuff even matters.

As you're working through Fantasy, Crime Fiction, and Science Fiction, ask yourself what your favorites were in these genres growing up and what your favorites are now. If you don't have any current loves, pick up one of the mentor texts mentioned in this section and test your palate. School and local librarians are amazing resources of popular genre fiction recommendations and can certainly help as well. Students care what we like, so it's important to find something praiseworthy in every genre and type of writing we study, whether you would ever choose to read or write that on your own.

At the end of these first three genre studies, what changes have you noticed in your students? What changes have they noticed in themselves? What can you celebrate as you head into your next genre-study cycle?

 Next Steps

Next Steps for Struggling or Reluctant Writers

Emphasize what students are producing in terms of word count and story ideas. Once when I was demo teaching, the host teacher pointed out a student and told me he would probably cry and get under his desk when I started talking about writing. The entire 45 minutes I kept an eye on the student, looking for signs of distress. He didn't write week 1 or week 2, but he was always paying attention and engaged (above his desk) which I took as a win. Suddenly week 3 he was writing along with everyone else, filling his wide-ruled notebook pages with big loopy handwriting. No, he wasn't writing even 100 words a class, but those 50-75 words were more than this student had ever produced independently. In teaching school, we learn to praise effort, and this is a key time to do so, not just for your struggling and reluctant writers, but for all your students. Writing is joyful and interesting, but it is also a work. Writing can make a person's brain feel tired, in a good way. Just as we strive to develop students into life-long readers, we can also grow life-long writers by giving them opportunities to experience the interaction of story magic and effort.

Next Steps for Gifted Writers

By this point, gifted writers are well down the road in at least one piece of long-form fiction if not several. Some gifted writers will have stopped listening to you after Fantasy or Crime because that's what they want to concentrate on. I let them know I'm fine with this option during any/all open writing time, but that I need them with me and participating during direct instruction of genre fiction. I explain, and I repeat this a lot, that my job is to teach them to write as many types of stories as possible. They may not want to do anything with that knowledge now, but it will likely come in handy down the road.

Some gifted writers might start to feel overwhelmed with too many ideas. For these students, they need a reminder that all ideas are the seeds of stories but can be left alone until the writer is ready to plant and grow them. Professional writers are often distracted by shiny new ideas and most of us, including me, keep a shiny new ideas file to come back to when we're ready to start something new.

At this point or soon-ish, you'll have at least a few of your highly capable writers stop writing or refuse to start because their writing does not immediately look professional, polished, or read as smoothly as their favorite mentor text. Be ready with ugly first drafts of your own work as well as that of famous professional writers. A great resource is *First Words: Early Writing From Favorite Contemporary Authors*, edited by Paul Mandelbaum (Algonquin Books of Chapel Hill, 1993). This book has early writing from Amy Tan, Michael Crichton, and Stephen King, among others. Just as with your struggling/reluctant writers, the emphasis should be on word count, knowledge acquired, and process. Publication comes later.

Humor, Horror, and Romance

 Overview

The next three genres provide an emotional experience for readers and writers, as well as a cerebral experience. While Humor, Horror, and Romance all stand alone as genres, they are also often blended with other genres. Sci-Fi Horror, for example, or Crime Comedy. Romance gets thrown in nearly everywhere, so we will cover both how to use Romance as the main plot structure and also as the B-story.

A middle school principal I respect very much recommended that teachers give the mental health team a heads up before starting this section of the book with students. I'm hopeful you know your class(es) well enough by now to make professional decisions about adjusting content as needed. Collaborating with your mental health colleagues around this work and letting students know you've done so, is not only smart, but great modeling for the neuro-diverse people in your classes.

If that paragraph gives you trepidation, I apologize, it's not meant to. Everything here has been structured and scaffolded to be taught to students as young as 3rd grade and as old 8th grade. This is more the veteran teacher in me reminding the newer teacher in me to pay extra attention to how students respond to fiction writing that requires emotional engagement.

*SEL (Social-Emotional Learning) note for this chapter: while ideas and cautions about supporting the social and emotional well-being of writers are sprinkled throughout the book, this section includes more explicit teaching around SEL because of the personal nature of what makes us laugh, scream, and sigh. These genres are where we can get into the critical writing strategy of engendering feelings in the reader. And these genres are also where we usually revisit writers' workshop guideline #3. Sometimes the writing gets so personal we reach out to the school mental health team for support.

Teaching Humor in Fiction aka Funny Stories

Of all the genres in the genre fiction section of this book, humor was the one that I learned how to teach by failing. Oh my gosh, teaching humor to 6th graders is hard! At least I thought it was at first because my students didn't get my jokes. At. All. Not regular classroom jokes, those were still fine, but the content I put in my earliest "how to write humor" lessons. And honestly, that right there is a kernel of how humor works. Teacher failures are hilarious to other teachers, as long as no one gets hurt. One time I was working with a group of teachers and talking about my struggle to teach younger students. A newer teacher said, "Tell us more about how you were sweating in front of those fourth graders. That's awesome." The perfectionist in me didn't think it was awesome. But do you see the set up? The picky, tidy everything-in-it's-place teacher failing in a messy, loud, go-with-the-flow classroom? Teacher humor. Gotta love it.

I found a picture of two people failing at playing tennis. Their rackets are broken, one is tangled in the net, and tennis balls are rolling everywhere. I show this and explain that in all the humor studies, the one common thing that made people laugh across all cultures was people you don't know getting a little bit hurt. That sounds cruel at first but think about pratfalls and sucker punches and slipping on a banana peel, classics of the humor cannon.

Beyond that, humor is personal to you, your childhood, your experiences, and your cultural context. Once I found that kernel of truth, my jokes landed better. I chose things that were funny for my students based on what I knew about them, rather than based on my contexts.

Humor Day 1 – Overview, Tropes, and Types of Humor

Warm-Up

Find images of strange products (like the Pet Petter) and choose five or six to display. (Searching social media for April Fool's Day prank products has yielded some fantastic finds, like Snackaging, edible packaging from Domino's and Nacho Cheesecake from The Cheesecake Factory.) The instructions are to write an advertisement for one product of their choice. Remind students about the content of advertisements: price, limited offer, most appropriate for, not recommended for, potential side effects, etc.

This is one of my favorite warm-ups and students who haven't written much sometimes come alive. Instead of the usual sharing routine, I group the students by the product they chose and have them share with each other. Then each group gets to pick their two favorites to be read aloud to the class. (I was demo teaching and a student's ad for pumpkin spice scented body wash made me spit laugh. Lesson learned. I no longer sip from my water bottle while students are sharing their advertisements.)

Mini-Lesson

Bring students back from the hilarity of their advertisements with the question, "What makes something funny to you?" The answers you need to get to are *context and connections*. (What makes something funny to you with columns for context and connections would make a great anchor chart for your study of humor.) Look for a single panel comic or use the April Fools' Day product, the kale milkshake from Sonic, with this question. The concept of a kale milkshake is only funny if you know what kale is and that it's been one of those trendy healthy ingredients that show up in seemingly everything.

One of my favorite mentor texts in this genre is *The Adventures of Captain Underpants* by Dav Pilkey (Scholastic, 1997). On the slide with favorite humor plot and character tropes, I use that book's cover. Additional mentor texts for humor are listed in Table 4.1 at the end of this section.

Favorite Comedy Plot Tropes:

- Mistaken Identity (could cross over to romance)
- Absurd Phobia
- Prank/Summer Camp Prank
- Hiding the Evidence (crime + humor)
- "Fish" Out of Water
- Fake Dating (romance + humor)
- Makeover
- Vacation Gone Wrong

Ask students to jot these in their notebooks and add examples of these from books, TV shows, and films. Give a gentle reminder to keep the examples within the PG/PG-13 boundary set previously. For older students, you might add *Taming of the Shrew* and the teen film adaptation, *10 Things I Hate about You* (Junger, Gil, director. Touchstone Pictures/Buena Vista Pictures, 1999) as a makeover example and *Twelfth Night* as a mistaken identity example. Because yes, Shakespeare used comedy tropes.

Favorite Comedy Character Tropes:

- Badly Battered Babysitter
- Absent Minded Professor
- Dumb and Gorgeous
- Bad Person plays Good Person on TV
- Wise Weirdo
- Mean Boss
- Creepy Old Person
- Sports Team Without Skills
- Arrogant Jerk
- Useless pet
- Hapless sidekick

On this slide you might use the movie poster for the Disney film, *The Mighty Ducks* (Herek, Stephen, director. Walt Disney Pictures/Buena

Vista Pictures, 1992). But before you start students working on examples, give a quick reminder about stereotypes. A humor writer can make fun of something or someone, but they have a responsibility to be sensitive to their audience and cultural norms as well. This is also a good time to remind your students that nothing we write can be based on people in the classroom.

Humor doesn't have specific setting tropes although the settings in humor tend toward the universal: schools, sports fields, stores, etc. Basically, something that's funny can be set pretty much anywhere as long as the audience can relate to the setting.

Beyond tropes, humor has categories and techniques that can be learned. The final segment of Day 1 is the technique of taking something to the extreme. This technique might be combined with the absurd phobia trope or with a running bit like a character's extreme love for pizza. (A running bit or running gag is a joke that's repeated throughout a piece and may also be funny due to the inappropriateness of when the joke/situation occurs.) For this I show an image from the Guinness Book of World Records, like the world's largest pizza. Then I use a clip from an early Jim Gaffigan routine where he's talking about how much he loves bacon ("King Baby." Netflix, 2008.) The humor is additive and he piles on for almost four minutes about all the things he loves about bacon cranking the audience up a little more with each fresh example. In horror, we might ask "what would make the situation worse?" In comedy, we might ask the same question, but with the understanding that worse = funnier. For example, getting embarrassed is bad. Getting embarrassed by your grandmother's dentures falling out in front of your crush is worse.

Humor Day 2 – Local Humor, Parody, and Weird Holidays

Warm-Up

Find a joke – a comic, a video, or an advertisement with humor specific to your area. My local news channel has a segment called, "The Most Colorado Thing We Saw Today." This segment gently pokes fun at very

Colorado things, like Ski-Lift Speed Dating. I also have a comic from the newspaper about summer watering restrictions – a very common situation during drought summers in Colorado. Other examples of local humor include the, "Nebraska, Honestly It's Not For Everyone" ad campaign. And the classic Wisconsin humor of the, "Manitowoc Minute" videos, created by Charlie Behrens in 2017. Hopefully you have something fun that's specific to your city or region.

Show several examples of local humor, including memes, and then invite the students to write one of their own that's specific to your town or even your school. Using memes here may open up another group of writers. I had a student who wasn't writing at all and after this lesson turned every subsequent assignment into memes. (Hey, they were spot on and he was finally writing something.) Here's the rationale I use for local humor: *local humor creates powerful rapport with the audience that can't be found anywhere else. Local humor creates community and is a great way to build connections with readers.* Whether they know to call them "in jokes" or not, most students have these kinds of jokes inside their friendship groups and/or family groups. Unfortunately, in jokes can be too limited to use in general writing, whereas local humor will capture a broader audience.

Mini-Lesson – Parody

On my definition slide, I have the movie poster for *Jaws* and then the parody poster for a fake movie, Paws, which shows a kitten in the position of the shark. The Paws poster is more amusing when you see it right next to the *Jaws* poster. That's the lesson of how to write parody in a nutshell, but we get to enjoy lots of fun examples in this segment.

> Parody definition: an imitation of the style of a particular writer, artist, or genre with deliberate exaggeration for comic effect.

Parody shows up across multiple types of writing including advertisements, books, songs, and films. Walk students through as many side-by-side comparisons as you have time for. I use:

Good Night Moon by Margaret Wise Brown (Harper & Brothers, 1947) and *Good Night iPad* by Ann Droyd (Blue Riders Press, 2011) available as books and videos.

"Happy"* by Pharrell Williams and "Tacky" by Weird Al Yankovic (videos).

"Hello" by Adele and "Snow" by Mary Morris (videos) *.

*If students decide to sing along, go with it.

Each of these has shot-for-shot and line-for-line matching. Making a good parody requires tremendous attention to detail. And the details are what make these things hilarious. Some of your students will want to linger on the genius of Weird Al. Mine certainly do. We ended up watching a Weird Al video of their choice as an earned reward on certain days for the last five minutes before the bell. One note of caution, not every song he parodies, in its original version, is ok for school.

Examples of looser, but still funny, parodies include the film *Space Balls* directed by Mel Brooks (Brooksfilms Metro-Goldwyn-Mayer/MGM UA Communications Co., 1987) and the picture book, *The Stinky Cheese Man and Other Fairly Stupid Tales* by Jon Scieszka and Lane Smith (Viking Books for Young Readers, 1992). As you close out this section, invite students to jot down some things they'd like to parody.

Writing Practice – Weird Holidays

Depending on where you live, and your internet feed, you might already get alerts like, "Today is National Pancake Day!" But a quick search for weird holidays will get you so many, much weirder opportunities. Find the list of your choice and post 10–15 examples of weird holidays with photos if possible.

For your students who aren't really into storytelling, per se, but like humor, weird holidays are the perfect opportunity to write one of the following:

- A fake newspaper story about how people in your city/town/region are celebrating Lumpy Rug Day on May 3.

- A how-to-celebrate guide for January 14, Dress Up Your Pet Day.

- A letter to the editor of your school paper about why the entire building should celebrate the Festival of Sleep.

Humor Day 3 – Dialog

It's certain that your students have been incorporating dialog in their snippets of writing so far. And it's also certain that they're making whimsical choices with punctuation and dialog tags. I think humor is a great place to practice dialog because much of what makes a character funny on the page is what they say, as much as what they do.

Warm-Up

On the board or a separate slide, I show students how the script version of dialog is laid out and instruct them to write in this format for now. I also usually add, "Copy this in your notebook just like this."

A:
B:
A:
B:
A:
B:

For today's warm-up, I use three to five photos from the internet treasure trove Awkward Family Photos (https://awkwardfamilyphotos.com/). The students may choose whichever of the photos they like and write about six lines of dialog. I always show an example of my own to emphasize that in this format, dialog tags are not needed.

A: My face hurts from smiling like this.
B: I think they said they had to adjust the lighting, that's why it's taking so long.
A: I will look terrible in this dress Mom picked out for me no matter what lighting they use.
B: Look at what Mom made me wear! A sailor suit!
A: Don't make me laugh! I'll lose a button on my matching sailor dress!
B: When I'm a parent I will never do this to my kids.

This day is also a bit of a deviation from the regular sharing routine because dialog needs to be read out loud. Pair students up and have them read each other's dialog, as in one partner reads A and one partner reads B.

Invite a pair or two to read the dialog out loud for the class. All of a sudden, your performers (including the ones you didn't know about) will sit up and pay attention.

Call students back to the lesson with the question, "How do real people sound when they talk?" I use a picture of someone eavesdropping for this slide. Most likely students won't have an answer for this. Explain that in real conversations, people use contractions, slang, uh, and um, interrupt each other, and trail off halfway through a thought. I have a funny gif from the movie *Valley Girl* that shows a snippet of the extremely slang heavy dialog.

Before you go any further, you need to add one more layer, which is the difference between dialog and dialect. For younger students, I use an excerpt from the picture book, *Flossie and the Fox* by Patricia McKissack (Dial Books, 1986). For older students, I use an excerpt from *The Adventures of Tom Sawyer* by Mark Twain (American Publishing Company, 1876). What you want them to see is that dialect is a technique to put words on the page in the way they sound as the character is speaking. These words may be spelled incorrectly to get to the pronunciation the writer wants the reader to hear. For example, a local greeting in New Orleans is, "Where y'at?" A common contraction in some parts of England is "init" – short for isn't it. "That's a terrible thing, init?" Don't linger on dialect too long. Rather, skim the examples and ask students to keep a look out for dialect choices by authors in their mentor texts this week. Use everything else in a professional-level manuscript, dialog inside quotation marks does not need to be grammatically correct or spelled correctly if the errors indicate how the character speaks.

Mini-Lesson

Some of your students will be thinking about how hard dialog is. Or that they don't know when to use it or how to use it. Some of the main reasons to use dialog in a piece of fiction are:

- Establish setting
- Set up conflict
- Foreshadowing
- Establish character and also character relationships

I have two favorite movie clips for this. You may have your own. Mine are the sword fight between the Man in Black and Inigo Montoya from film version of *The Princess Bride* (Reiner, Rob, director. Act III Communications/ Twentieth Century Fox, 1987). The other is the early sword fight between Captain Jack Sparrow and Will Turner from the first Pirates of the Caribbean film, *The Curse of the Black Pearl* (Bruckheimer, Jerry, et al. Walt Disney Pictures/Buena Vista Pictures, 2003). Why sword fights? Well, because fight scenes should always move the story forward *and* in both these scenes the viewer learns a great deal about the characters before, during, and after the fight. I like to model the combination of conversation and action. Beginning writers may write dialog where the characters are standing and doing nothing and then an action scene where characters are fighting but not talking.

Put the A: B: format on the board or screen again and explain that we're going to continue practicing dialog. Say, "Please write the most boring dialogue you can." This is tricky but what you're doing is building confidence. Ask students who think they have boring dialog to raise their hands. Their first attempts usually aren't quite boring enough. I often have to say, "No, I get a sense of character with this. Try to make it worse and more boring." Or, "Hm, I sense some conflict in this dialogue, so try harder to make it boring." (Double top secret: students will be revising on the spot to make their dialog more boring. Do NOT point this out.) Have students read the boring dialog with a partner and have a few volunteer pairs perform the boring dialog for the class. Clap enthusiastically for the boring dialog.

Say, "Okay, now add two distinct characters. Make these two very different people, like an English Butler and a Professional Wrestler. Or a Pirate and a Princess." Students should still be writing in the A:B: format, but now they're trying to get a sense of character on the page. You don't have to write the boring dialog, but you should try the character dialog for yourself. For this I use a picture of a poofy Pomerian and a husky Bulldog and I display the imaginary dialog I wrote to go along with the photo. Based on how I wrote it, the students always guess correctly which lines belong to the Pomeranian and which to the Bulldog.

Go through the pairing and sharing routine. Include performing, if you have time.

The last round of this is adding conflict. Say, "Keep these two characters and now make them stuck in an elevator." Other conflict options: only one piece of dessert remaining and both characters want it, Character A is hiding something from Character B, Character B has a secret crush on Character A, etc.

Again, depending on time, pair-share-perform. Students will love doing this. Even your non-writers, non-performers will participate.

The final trick is to take dialog written in the A:B: format and transform it to the format most commonly found in fiction. Don't rush this. If you don't have time today, this can definitely go to the next class. What I do is take my Pomerian/Bulldog dialog and I add all the tags. Another option beyond a plain tag is to add an action for the character before, during, or after speaking.

> Definition – Dialog Tag – Also referred to as an attribution, a **dialog tag** is a small phrase either before, after, or in between the actual **dialog** itself, like "he said."

Two teacher things:

1. Adverbs weaken strong verbs – try to avoid them. It is not necessary to write "she shouted loudly" because shouting implies loudly just as running implies quickly.

2. "Said" is alive and well. If students aren't sure what to use for a dialog tag, they should use "said." Professional writers use "said" for 50% or more of dialog tags because it disappears into the story and doesn't distract the reader. All those other words like growled, screeched, muttered, etc., are distracting.

Here's the final draft of my Pomeranian and Bulldog dialog with tags added.

A: Allessandra trotted to the bone and took a delicate sniff. "This smells delightful."

B: "It smells like plastic bacon and plastic cheeseburger," Bruno said. "But together. In a bone shape."

A: "I'm sure whoever left this here had exquisite taste and enjoyed pâté and carpaccio. Not bacon and cheeseburger." She gave a tiny, yippy-sounding laugh.

B: Leaning forward, Bruno inhaled. As he did so, a thick tendril of drool spiraled toward the bone. "Yummy."

A: "Bruno, no!" Allesandra slapped her tiny paw against the bone and knocked it away. But alas, she was too late. The drool landed with a thick splat.

The Longest Drive of My Life by Cody S., 5th Grade

I was planning to go to Kansas to see my family and have a fun time. Little did I know I would be taking my dog on a ten hour drive! We were late to board Millie, and at one point we just gave up because all the borders were full for the holidays. We should have known this was going to happen because if you're late to the party don't expect a seat.

Millie isn't a "regular" dog. As a matter of fact, she doesn't even act like a dog. And I'm pretty sure her spirit animal is a cat. Why? The answer is simple, she acts like one. She's mean, she does what she wants when she wants, and she's just flat out evil. Another thing is I don't like cats and I could say the same about Millie, a mean Wheaten Terrier who always snaps at me, and my siblings too. What I'm trying to say is that I don't like Millie, and when I thought her being in the car with us couldn't get any worse, it did; when I found out she would be riding in the back… with me.

I could have said Millie was weird before we went on the drive, but now after being in the car with her for 10 hours I can assure you she's weird. She stood up in the car for more than half the time we were in it. Her breath also smells, especially when she pants and whines, and she panted and whined for so long that my mom finally stopped the car and walked Millie around. After that, the whining and panting stopped and we were back on the road.

Millie was getting on my nerves, but then she threw up on Olivia, and that's when she started to grow on me. The times she wasn't standing, she'd sit down next to me. The times she wasn't throwing up on Olivia, she was cuddled up next to me. The times she wasn't with me because I blocked off the path, she was with me. When we dropped off Millie at my grandparent's house I thought silently to myself, "Yeah, we can be friends."

Table 4.1 Mentor Texts Humor

Genre	Type of Book	Title	Author
Humor	Picture book	17 Things I'm Not Allowed to Do Anymore	Jenny Offill
	Picture book	Interrupting Chicken	David Ezra Stein
	Picture book	Finders Keepers	Keiko Kasza
	Early Reader	Knights of the Kitchen Table	Jon Scieszka
	Early Reader	Captain Underpants	Dav Pilkey
	Middle Grade	Hoot	Carl Hiaasen
*Graphic novel	Middle Grade	I'm Ok	Patti Kim
	Middle Grade	Millicent Min, Girl Genius	Lisa Yee
	Middle Grade	Diary of a Wimpy Kid	Jeff Kinney
*Sci-fi	Young Adult	Grasshopper Jungle	Andrew Smith
	Young Adult	Angus, Thongs, and Full Frontal Snogging	Louise Rennison
*Crime	Young Adult	The Disreputable History of Frankie Landau-Banks	E. Lockhart

Horror Lesson Ideas

Know what else is personal. What scares you. Through trial and error, I realized teaching humor and horror in consecutive weeks made the most sense because the techniques to write each of these types of stories are related. The concept of "find the universal in the personal" might seem out there for younger students, but I promise you, it is not. As with science fiction, some teachers shy away from teaching horror, but making space for writing about scary things is important. The lesson plans for horror have the most variations available, however, so you will have options to adjust for your specific students.

Please don't skip the horror genre because it upsets you. No matter their age, you will have students who prefer to view, read, play and write scary stories. Also, later when students are writing opinion pieces about things that are scary in real life, like toxic waste in the oceans or animal testing, they will have this skill set, the horror writing skill set, to lean on.

Horror Day 1 – Set Up and Setting

Before you begin studying horror as a genre, make sure you know which of your students are worried about this. Some people are very sensitive about scary things. This might be a good time to rearrange seats so that those students are closest to the classroom door and can quietly slip out, if needed. That being said, I've never had a student leave, but I think the offer gave them needed comfort and support.

Warm-Up

Display a picture of a spooky house. The prompt is: *write the opening to a spooky story with the house as the narrator.* I purposely chose the word spooky because that's less upsetting to your more sensitive students than words like "scary" or "horror." If possible, find an audio clip of wind and have that playing in the background. Wind is a sound that makes the primate part of our brains uncomfortable. As students get ready to write to the opener, remind them to include all five senses as they're describing the spooky house. Sound and smell can be triggers that "something isn't right about this place." The genre is called "Horror," but it encompasses a wide range of emotions from low-level dread all the way up to stark terror.

Mini-Lesson

After students share out, you might choose to show the trailer for the film *Monster House* (Kenan, Gil, director. Sony Pictures, 2006). For older students, you might show the trailer for the 1999 version of *The Haunting* (de Bont, Jan, director. DreamWorks Pictures). This one was rated PG-13 and was critically panned, but full of tropes. Take a few minutes to capture the most common descriptors for scary houses. Some of your students might have visited the Haunted Mansion attraction at one of the Disney parks. Invite those students to talk about the spooky elements included in the line queue and the entrance hall and the room/elevator. You can also find walk-throughs of this ride on YouTube.

Just as writers and filmmakers use setting to indicate genre and get the audience ready to be spooked, we are going to start with setting to warm-up our thinking about scary things.

Ask students, where are other places people might be a little bit scared? Or truly frightened? You'll get a wide range of answers, but you should hear themes around being trapped and also of being in a place with imminent danger, like an abandoned factory full of rusty equipment. You might also get answers related to death and ghosts, like hospitals and cemeteries. Depending on the range of backgrounds and experiences in your group, you might get a few surprising answers. This is a moment to model your support of student risk-taking and sharing personal things.

Show this list of Horror Setting Tropes and invite students to add ideas that might be missing.

- Evil Lair
- Summer Camp
- Cemetery

- Cabin in the Woods
- Perfectly ordinary and not abandoned place (sometimes the most frightening)

The second half of the list is places that are scarier when they're run-down and abandoned:

- Hospital
- Warehouse
- School
- Apartment Building
- Mansion
- Resort
- Military Base

Ask students to copy both lists into their notebooks and to put a star by at least two settings that interest them.

Next show an Abandoned Places slideshow. Several of these exist and can be found via a quick internet search or you can make your own. Direct students to jot down adjectives and descriptive phrases that come to mind as they view each image. Again, lean into the idea of including all five senses. When a human (in this case, a character in a story) is on the edge of "flight, fight, or freeze" certain senses shift into high alert. This is one of the reasons why darkness is can be frightening, because it disrupts our reliance on visual information.

Ask students to look back at their opening writing on the spooky house. In horror, the setting can be an actual character. Or the setting can be so significant that it feels like a character and if you took the story out of that setting (my favorite the Great Dismal Swamp, for example), the story wouldn't work anymore. Your closing writing for this class should be an invitation to work on developing a setting for a scary story.

Modification for the horror-averse – to make notes about how setting can work as a character in *other* types of stories, like a romance set in New York City or a quest set in Middle Earth.

Extension for horror-enthusiasts – make notes about how settings can show the reader more facets of the villain, like the lair of the Grinch.

Horror Day 2 – Characters and Monsters

Between the end of writing class yesterday and the beginning of writing class today, find a moment to check in privately and discretely with your students who were worried about studying horror.

Warm-Up

On the screen, show a set of monster/villain images from popular scary movies. You might have the "other mother" from *Coraline*, some of the zombies from *ParaNorman*, any old Dracula film, a ghost from *Ghost Busters*, a shark from *The Meg*, etc. Choose your combination based on the ages/needs of your students. Generally, older students want to see characters from more intense shows, games, and films, but not always. The prompt is to choose a character to write a little more about. They can choose Dracula's point of view OR they can write from the point of view of someone seeing Dracula for the first time.

Selick, Henry, director. *Coraline*. Universal Pictures, 2009. Based on the book *Coraline* by Neil Gaiman.

Fell, Sam and Chris Butler, directors. *ParaNorman*. Laika/Focus Features, 2012.

Reitman, Ivan. *Ghostbusters*. Columbia Pictures, 1984.

Turteltaub, Jon, director. *The Meg*. Gravity Pictures/Warner Brothers Pictures, 2018.

After sharing out, bring students back with the question: "When is a monster a villain?" You might use images of both Sully and Randall from *Monsters, Inc.* to go along with this question. Not all of your students will know the film *Monsters, Inc.* (Docter, Pete, director. Walt Disney Pictures/Buena Vista Pictures, 2001), so make sure to request additional examples. You're looking for answers about both context, motivation, and behavior of the monster. Sometimes a shark is just hungry, for example.

[A word of caution: this is often a moment when I am shocked (on the inside) by what level of rated R horror films and rated M games my students have been exposed to. When someone brings up an example that's way out of line for school and the age of the group, acknowledge it but say something along the lines of *yes, but that's one we can't talk about in 5th grade*, or whatever feels comfortable for you. You don't want to invalidate the student's experience, but you also don't want angry calls and emails because one of your students terrified half the class with a graphic summary of *The Shining* by Stephen King, either the book (Doubleday, 1977) or the film (Kubrick, Stanley, director. Warner Brothers, 1980).

Mini-Lesson

Today's practice is about how to plan a monster story. I generally stick to supernatural or natural monsters. Human monsters are often too frightening and too realistic for my students. If your students really want to write about a human monster, steer them toward examples like Lord Farquad from *Shrek* (Adamson, Andrew and Vicky Jenson, directors. Dreamworks, 2001) or Moriarty from *Sherlock Holmes*. (Doyle, Arthur Conan. "The Adventure of the Final Problem." *The Memoirs of Sherlock Holmes*, Strand Magazine, 1893.) Mentor texts to support the study of the Horror genre are listed in Table 4.2 at the end of this section.

Ask students to write the steps down in their notebooks.

Step 1: Introduce the monster
- Where is the monster supposed to be? Is that different from where it is now?
- Who sees it?
- How does the character who sees the monster feel about the monster? (*This last part is perhaps the most important. If the character is terrified for her life in the first sentence, the story will proceed much differently than if the character is amused or irritated.*)

Step 2: Show the world of the monster
- What kind of world is it?
- Do monsters appear all the time?
- Is the human world under siege by monsters?

- Or is this a regular world with a very personal monster? *To answer this question, you'll also need to figure out the main character's place in the world.*

Step 3: Describe this kind of monster, even if it's the only one of its kind

- What does the monster look like?
- How does it move?
- Does the monster communicate? If so, how?
- Why has the monster appeared (to this character) at this time?

Step 4: Match the monsters to the main character or if the monster is the main character, determine who/what is this monster's antagonist. Monsters and their opposing characters should be well matched. *Figure out the character's life, problems, and conflicts that existed before the monster arrived. If you make the character's personal conflict part of the story from the beginning, the monster will naturally be viewed as part of that conflict.*

Step 5: Additional character tropes to consider:

- Ancient Evil
- Last Girl
- Vengeful Spirit
- Creepy Doll
- Crusty Caretaker
- Skilled Hunters of X
- Mad Scientist
- Survivor of "the last time this happened"

Day 3: Horror Story Starters and Techniques

The more I wrote, the more I wanted to learn about the craft of writing and my interests shifted to "how" questions. With horror, I really wanted to dig into HOW mere words on a page had me sweating, heart pounding, and dry-mouthed on an otherwise quiet, sunny, pleasant day when I was not in any mortal danger whatsoever. *Because that's magic, the special magic created by the right words in the right order. Your students want to know the secret of that magic as well.*

Warm-Up

Choose a series of mildly creepy photographs. I use these four from Unsplash.com: an axe in a basket, hands clutching the edge of a cliff, a cabin shrouded in fog, and a person looking at a map by the side of the road. The prompt is: *put these photographs in an order that makes sense to you and write the opening lines of the story they tell. Then rearrange the photographs and decide if and how much that changes the story. Write a new opening sentence for the new arrangement.* I like these images because they are not immediate to the urban and suburban settings where I work. If you're teaching in a rural community, you might choose more urban images to keep the scary stuff from being too close to home.

 ## *Mini-Lesson*

After the sharing routine, bring students back with the question: If a story isn't scary is it still considered horror? What you will likely get is both *yes* and *no*. And also, *it depends*. What scares each of us is personal and individualized, at least to a certain extent.

From here generate a list of common fears – you can get fancy by using the Latin names of the fears. One article I found groups the most common phobias into four categories: Natural Environment, Animals, Medical Treatment, Situations. Thinking of these categories might help your students think of a few more. Don't spend too much time on this. Just use a little time to get ideas going because a character with a phobia is a great way to start a scary story.

- Agoraphobia – fear of open spaces.
- Arachnophobia – fear of spiders.
- Anatidaephobia – fear of being watched by a duck (I always mention this because it's so interesting).
- Claustrophobia – fear of enclosed spaces.
- Coulrophobia – fear of clowns.
- Ophidiophobia – fear of snakes.

- Pteromerhanophobia – fear of flying.
- Triskaidekaphobia – fear of the number 13 (often a word for the National Spelling Bee).

Once you have a good list, ask students to jot down a few thoughts about how they might react if they had to confront one of their personal fears. Ask them to be specific, if possible, about how they might feel physically – such as churning stomach, limbs heavy or frozen, etc. Let them know this will not be a time for sharing out.

Naming phobias can turn into a fun vocabulary game/extension if you've been studying Greek and Latin roots as a class.

Technique 1: Establish Normal and Then Twist It in a Scary Way

Think about everyday activities and throw in an upsetting element, such as finding a severed ear on the way to school. You will get a reaction on this one and students will want to immediately go to something supernatural. But that's not what this technique is about, an ear is still a "normal" thing, but "severed" changes the situation, as does the context of a person's typical walk to school.

Technique 2: Start with the Character in Trouble

Begin the story by trapping your character(s) in a confined space like a cellar, a coffin, an abandoned hospital, an island, or an abandoned town. This will create an immediate conflict or threat to the character(s) and set your story up with immediate tension or suspense. On this slide I have a photo of an abandoned playground. I talk about how many teachers have a fear of leaving a student behind on a field trip. Some students think it might be fun to be left behind, if it was a fun field trip, but often places, like museums, stop being cool and get a little creepy after closing time. Museums have extensive security features, including timed locks. What if your character hears the locks click and knows the doors won't unlock until sunrise…

Technique 3: Create Extreme Emotions – A Key to the Horror Genre

Shock

This is the classic jump-scare and the main reason people say they don't like scary stuff. People hate being so startled they literally jump in their seats. What's worse is the embarrassed feeling that often comes immediately after jumping in one's seat. As a writer, you might have one or two of these in a story like a huge surprise or a splash of gore, but shock is a technique to use lightly. Have students pause here to make a few notes about where shock might fit with the story ideas they are jotting down.

Paranoia

The sense that something is not quite right can unnerve the reader, make them doubt their own surroundings, and when used to its full effect, make the reader doubt even their own beliefs or ideas of the world. This type of fear is great for slow tension-building and psychological horror stories. Usually paranoia starts with small details the character and therefore the reader can shrug off. But as the details accumulate, the emotion grows more intense. Pause here for students to jot down notes about how they might use paranoia to increase the tension in the story they're playing with.

Dread

Dread is the horrible sense that something bad is going to happen. Dread works well when the reader connects deeply to the story and begins to care enough about the characters to fear something bad is going to happen to them. Inspiring dread in a reader is tricky as the story will need to do a lot of work to keep the reader engaged and involved, but it creates a powerful connection between the character(s) and the reader. On this slide I have a photo of an open closet door. As a child, and mostly now, I can't sleep if the closet door is open. Dread in a story is often about facing that scary place or the character putting themselves in the situation that worries them the most.

Recipe for a Horror Story

- Create likable or relatable characters
- Blend in their "normal" life
- Add something wrong, upsetting, or terrible
- Add something worse
- Result: Character does or does not vanquish monster, situation, etc.

More story ideas:

- A girl wakes up to find a little boy sitting on her bed, claiming to be her younger brother – but she never had one.
- A person wakes up to find their family gone and the doors and windows boarded up with no way to escape.
- A person afraid of snakes is shipwrecked on an island covered with them.
- A young brother and sister find an old door in their basement that wasn't there before.
- A boy realizes that his family has been replaced by aliens. (Horror + sci-fi)
- A bank robber steals from the small town bank that holds the riches of witches.
- A family buys a cheap house only to discover that an old cemetery is their back yard.
- A family on a boat trip stumbles upon an old pirate ship.
- Children discover a deep, dark well in the woods – an old ladder leads down into it.

"Hallway" by Sadie P. 6th grade

Hi. I'm your daily newspaper girl. I'm 13. Today I'm passing out newspapers to the 1800's museum, where nobody has gone in 1 decade. The manager had told me to go this morning. I've arrived. There's a cracked sign that says, "Done For". Caution tape surrounds the large building. I'm not surprised this place went out of business. It is far from the city. I tear down the caution tape to get inside. The doors are mammoth-like. It is as if this is a crime. The door is open. I walk inside, and there are all these statues. Creepy statues. Considering there is zero light, and I have to use my phone flash.

The door shuts completely, and it makes a loud, unpleasant noise. There are all these old, ancient, statues from Eastern and Western Europe. Honestly, it is really creepy to look at. I look down the dark, mysterious, hallway. The mailbox is standing right there at the end of the hall. I know I'm 13, but right now, I'm actually a bit frightened to deliver the mail.

I hesitantly walk to the mailbox, and all of a sudden, the museum manager walks out of another hallway, to the right of me. He gives me a genuinely friendly smile, and walks off into the distance behind me. I hear the doors open and shut, which gives me the chills, for some reason. I begin to speed walk to the mailbox. "Everything will be fine," I think. I open the almost broken mailbox, and slide the pack of letters inside. I take a large exhale, and feel relieved. I begin to walk to the entrance. Finally.

I try to open the door, but it is locked. "Maybe it's just jammed?" I thought. I try to push harder. Nothing moves. Uh, what now? I decide to text the manager, but there's no signal here. That's odd. I tell myself that everything is gonna be fine. There's still no light in here. Not even windows.

Table 4.2 Mentor Texts Horror

Horror	Type of Book	Title	Author
	Picture book	*How to Make Friends with a Ghost*	Rebecca Green
	Picture book	*Creepy Carrots!*	Aaron Reynolds
	Early reader	*Spooky and Spookier: 4 American Ghost Stories*	Lori Haskins Houran
	Middle grade	*Scary Stories to Tell in the Dark*	Alvin Schwartz
	Middle grade	*City of Ghosts*	Victoria Schwab
	Middle grade	*The Last Kids on Earth*	Max Brallier
	Middle grade	*Small Spaces*	Katherine Arden
	Middle grade	*The Screaming Staircase*	Jonathan Stroud
	Young adult	*Rot and Ruin*	Jonathan Maberry
	Young adult	*Five Midnights*	Ann Dávila Cardinal

Romance

Intro and Overview

Romance is almost as hard a sell as horror is but while student writers won't admit they're interested in the techniques used by romance writers, secretly, they are. For your youngest or least mature students, however, you might consider skipping the first mini-lesson of this section and going to the imbedded romance/friendship arc techniques.

One of the difficult parts is that while it is a billion-dollar industry, romance as a genre and romance writers still draw criticism and scorn from other, usually literary, writers. Romance is often dismissed as formulaic and "paint by the numbers" fiction.

Remind your students that all genre fiction is formulaic. That's the point. Genre fiction is a great place to learn how to write because each genre already has a starting line, lane lines, and a finish line. And while romance stands alone as a very successful genre, with its own large section in most libraries and bookstores, it is also a set of story techniques that get mixed into nearly every other genre as well.

- Middle Grade romance is usually about crushes and/or friendships.
- Young Adult romance usually goes beyond crushes into dating, kissing, etc.

Romance Day 1 – Tropes

Warm-Up

Choose one of the following dialog pairs to start a scene:

"I saved your life!"
"You pushed me off a building!"

"That's disgusting. You're lucky you're cute."
"Thanks, I think."

"Hey, you dropped this book."
"No, I didn't. Wait…that's my grandmother's book of spells. How did you get it?"

"Before I leave on this quest, I would ask a token of your favor."
"This is my lucky pebble. I hope it will bring you luck as well."

On this slide but also on other slides in the romance section, I use images of all different sorts of couples. You have no way of knowing all the interests and secret wishes of your students so demonstrating a true openness to many types of pairings is important. (Think about how most primary teachers strive to have a collection of picture books showing every configuration of family. It's like that, but with couples.) Anime offers a host of gender fluid characters if you're not sure where to look. I generally choose pairings from popular fiction, cartoons, etc. Just like with the books about all different types of families, you're showing students possibilities as well as building their sensitivity and awareness. Rick Riordan's books, especially the later series' like *The Trials of Apollo* (Disney-Hyperion, 2016), offer many options for how a wide range of romance and crush options can show up on the page. Additional options for mentor texts for Romance are listed in Table 4.3 given at the end of this section.

Mini-Lesson

After the sharing out routine (and yes, some sneaky dialog practice) move right into romance tropes. Show the following list and ask students to copy it into their notebooks. They should also star or underline their favorites.

- Friends to dating
- Enemies to dating
- Sibling's best friend
- Second chance
- Next door neighbor you've always known and suddenly realize you have a crush on
- Mysterious stranger (often with other worldly powers)
- Starcrossed (Romeo & Juliet trope)

- Fake relationship
- Hero+Regular person
- Instalove
- Love Triangle
- Cyrano
- Pygmalion (the Makeover)

It's less likely that your students will know the source material for the *Cyrano* and *Pygmalion* tropes. I give mine some background information and then I share examples I wrote to illustrate each trope. The *Pygmalion* trope, aka the Makeover trope, is extremely common, so students should recognize it with just a touch of explanation.

Cyrano de Bergerac by Edmond Rostand (1897) was a play about a man who was a brave and skilled soldier as well as very intelligent and witty. But he had a HUGE nose. Rather than risk rejection from the woman he loved, Roxanne, he wrote notes and pretty speeches for a very handsome but far less intelligent soldier, Christian, to use to woo Roxanne. And this works. Roxanne marries Christian. *Spoiler: Roxanne doesn't find out the truth until the very end of the play when Christian is long dead and Cyrano is dying. The film version of this, called *Roxanne* and starring Steve Martin, doesn't end on such a dire note. But it's from the days prior to the PG-13 rating. Having shown this to a class I can tell you it's a PG film that would definitely have a PG-13 rating by current standards. (Schlepsi, Fred, Director. Columbia Pictures, 1987.)

Pygmalion is a play by George Bernard Shaw (1913). The musical and film version, *My Fair Lady* (Lerner and Loewe, 1956) is based on this play. The *Pygmalion* trope is also the Makeover trope in which the creator falls in love with their creation.

Below are the examples I wrote for each

Cyrano trope:

Jordan opened her locker and peered around it to watch the cluster of bas-ketball players standing nearby. Her stomach flipped over and her lips went dry every time she saw her crush, Trey. But she still watched him with his teammates each morning. Her best friend, Shayla, walked up to wish Trey and the rest of the guys good luck in their game. Shayla was so good at talking to people. Jordan shook her head and forced herself to look away. She was hopeless. If only Shayla could do the talking for her.

Pygmalion trope:

On his 16th birthday, Angelo's grandmother pulled him aside and gave him an envelope with a thousand dollars, ten hundred dollar bills inside. "To make a wish come true," she whispered with a secret smile. What did Angelo wish more than anything? To be noticed by the prettiest, smartest girl in his high school, Taylor Flores-Gonzalez. He was a good guy. He got good grades. Wasn't bad looking either. But he was a social nobody.

As Angelo sat on the lifeguard chair at his summer job that June, he over-heard one of the other guards talking about a car he wanted to buy. "Just need another grand," the guy said. "They're keeping it for me. A sweet little Subaru."

The guy talking was Mr. Popularity and in the same group as Taylor. Would a thousand dollars buy "how to be cool" lessons and get him a spot at the popular lunch table? Only one way to find out.

Romance scenes to try:

- First meeting
- First date
- One of the characters realizes this relationship has the potential to be something special
- A play fight turns into a real fight
- An outside person or situation does something damaging to the relationship
- One of the characters makes a grand gesture to apologize/demonstrate renewed commitment to the relationship

Romance Day 2 – The Friendship Arc and Romance as the B-story

You will have students who want to write stories about the trials and tribulations of friendship, or possibly a buddy comedy. Some of the romance tropes will work perfectly for these types of stories as well. The underlying similarity is the journey to true connection between individuals whether the result is platonic or romantic.

Warm-Up

Post a picture or several pictures of two people sharing food or maybe whispering together, like they're sharing a secret. Prompt: *Describe the first time two people destined to be best friends met. Be sure to include what they liked about each other and how they knew they would become friends.*

In romance, this type of scene is called the "meet-cute," but it definitely works for friendship arcs as well.

Mini-Lesson

Romance tropes that could work as Friendship Arc tropes:

- Enemies to friends
- Second chance
- Mysterious stranger
- Hero + regular person
- Fake friends (as in the characters have to fake a friendship for a *plot reason*)

A book about friendship that follows a romance pattern would include the following:

- A meet cute
- Fun and games – aka the friends enjoying stuff together
- Struggles and challenges to the friendship (internal and external)
- An ending that shows a deep commitment to the friendship going forward

Romance as the B-story

The B-story is the secondary story in a novel, often used to underscore the themes of the primary story. When romance is used as the B-story, it can offer "catch your breath" moments or much needed laughs in heavier, more intense plots. Romance also adds **plot hooks** to keep people reading, adds **stakes** for a main character who needs to save the_____ and now has to also protect a love interest, and can contribute to the overall **change arc of a main character**. "I used to be so focused on my job doing ____, but now I also care about your puppy and you. I see things differently now."

Plot hooks are the small, but compelling story threads that keep a reader reading. Romance almost always adds that touch of "ooh, are they going to get together?" Many people, me included, will turn pages just to find out. Even when the romance is deeply back-burnered for the main plot line, as in the *Percy Jackson and the Olympians* books by Rick Riordan, readers are eager to see Percy defeat the monsters, but also, they're curious if he and Annabeth are going to end up as a couple.

Stakes are what you use to kill vampires AND stakes are what keep the main character in the fight/conflict/storyline. Stakes are about what the main character has to gain if they complete the main task, which in romance, might be competing for the title of prom queen. Stakes are also about what the main character might lose if they don't complete the task. You saw this word earlier in the Crime Fiction lessons. In Crime Fiction, stakes are often life or death. In romance, the main character isn't often risking death, but is has to *feel like* they are. Anyone who has stood in front of an entire auditorium full of their peers to give a speech or perform a new dance routine knows this exact feeling.

Change Arc is one of the few teacher and teacher school things that is familiar here. Usually, at least one character undergoes a significant change as a result of the challenges and tasks set before them in the story. In romance, this is definitely true. Being in a strong, healthy, supportive relationship (romantic or platonic) changes a person for the better.

The first *Shrek* film (Adamson, Andrew and Vicky Jenson, directors. Dreamworks, 2001) is an excellent mentor text for both romance as the B-story and the Friendship Arc. One could argue the main plot of *Shrek* is what he tells us it is: Shrek wants to get his swamp back and he wants all the fairy tale creatures to leave. The main plot follows the classic quest structure. Donkey joining Shrek on the quest is the Friendship Arc story-line. This follows the very pleasing trope of two opposites, or at least starkly different personalities, learning to become friends. The third layer is the mutual attraction between Shrek and Fiona. As Shrek changes and becomes more vulnerable, the romance story line becomes more important than the quest. For younger students who might think that romance is icky, they usually can see the point that even if they would never want such a thing for themselves, they want Shrek to be happy with Fiona in the end. Incidentally, for writers who want to work on subplots, the first *Shrek* film is a great mentor text as well.

Before you close for the day, ask students to play around with ideas where a subtle romance could be the B-story in the crime or fantasy or science fiction they're writing. Don't be surprised at how many of them were already heading in this direction. Or, if your students are clearly only wanting to write friendship stories, have them think about genre fiction where the development of a new, meaningful friendship is the B-story. One of the best examples might be Frodo and Sam in the *Lord of the Rings* trilogy (Tolkien, J. R. R. *The Fellowship of the Ring*. 1st ed., George Allen & Unwin, 1954), but not all students know that one.

Romance Day 3

Rather than a new mini-lesson for Day 3, invite students to play with one of the following scenes in their notebook or to add into their ongoing piece of fiction:

- A meet cute
- Fun and games – aka the friends/possible romantic interests enjoying stuff together
- Struggles and challenges to the friendship or romance (internal and external)
- An ending that shows a deep commitment to the friendship or romance going forward

One note regarding "and they lived happily ever after." In Young Adult romance, the goal is not for the two characters to be married at the end of the story. The goal is "happy for now" and often ends with a big romantic moment like Prom or a different, high stakes, formal occasion. A great example is the last five minutes of the film *Clueless* (Heckerling, Amy, director. Paramount Pictures, 1995) where the main character, Cher, explains exactly how gross it is (to her) that teenagers would get married.

Table 4.3 Mentor Texts Romance

Romance	Type of Book	Title	Author
*Graphic novel	Middle grade	*Drama*	Raina Telgemeier
	Middle grade	*Hurricane Child*	Kacen Callender
	Middle grade	*Donut Go Breaking My Heart: A Wish Novel*	Suzanne Nelson
	Young adult	*Frankly in Love*	David Yoon
	Young adult	*You Should See Me in a Crown*	Leah Johnson
	Young adult	*Don't Date Rosa Santos*	Nina Moreno
	Young adult	*The Replacement Crush*	Lisa Brown Roberts
	Young adult	*To All the Boys I've Loved Before*	Jenny Han

Ask Your Students

Ask your students if they're having fun. All my writers love the humor lessons and they usually end up loving the horror and romance lessons too. Ask them to count up all the words they've written in the past week. Ask if they're surprising themselves.

Week six of genre fiction is a good time to pause and reflect. Have students look back to the first pages in their notebooks and compare their writing to now. I wish I could be with you to see the smiles of wonder. Elementary students will be blown away to have 400, 700, and 900 words. A hundred is a lot of something after all.

Middle school students should count both what's in their notebooks and what they've typed (most electronic document software has a tool feature to count words). Generally by now they're producing word counts in the thousands. Turns out writing every day generates big piles of words.

Ask how writing feels in their bodies, which might be an unusual question. Do their shoulders feel tight or loose? What about their hands? How are they breathing? Most of the time you'll get responses that add up to happy and relaxed. Tell them to remember how this feels, to remember that writing can create that inner bubble of joy. Don't tell them this is a feeling they'll need to find on the days the writing is harder and less fun. At least not yet. Instead spend a few minutes reflecting and celebrating together.

Ask Yourself

Ask yourself, what are you noticing in your own writing and in your stance about reading and writing Humor, Horror, and Romance? Are you having fun? Do you feel like you're eating birthday cake every day? (Or indulging in some other guilty pleasure?) Sometimes teachers feel pressure to only read and discuss texts that are full of lofty ideas and themes that uplift humanity. Genre fiction doesn't have the same reputation as literary fiction in this regard. HOWEVER, the themes of friendship, courage, doing the right thing even when it's the hard thing, etc., can be found in all genres of fiction.

As you're going through the mini-lessons for Humor, Horror, and Romance check in with your students often. Ask how they are, maybe increase the time allotted for conferring. Again, most of them will be fine, happy, ready to write. But a few might need some individual attention from you and/or a colleague from the mental health team. Strong readers experience a book as a "mind movie." Writers also have the mind-movie experience, but while they're putting the words on the page. Every writer I know has admitted to crying or paranoia or elation based entirely on what the fictional characters in the fictional world they've created are going through. I remember the first time I cried writing a scene and how strange I felt afterward, crying over people and a situation I invented. Reassuring your students "fiction isn't real" doesn't work and doesn't help. In the moment, the brain experiences the emotions as though they were real.

Because the work of these three genres, especially humor and horror, is the work of finding the universal in the personal, your students are going to have lots of connections to the content. Get ahead of this and ask the class to think about the best ways to invite personal connections into writing workshop without getting sidetracked from the day's mini-lesson and practice. Another reason you want to put this out to everyone is that by now you probably know which students always have a connection to whatever you might be learning, and which students never volunteer that sort of information.

One thought is to have a side-project, maybe on a chart or a bulletin board, or as a separate folder in your digital classroom called "Fact is Stranger than Fiction." Students could write out (or dictate) true, personal stories that are related to the genres of humor, horror, and romance. You would need to screen these, of course, and confer about them, but this gives a respectful space to the upswell of personal stories that will come out of this work.

After teaching six genres of fiction, how has student engagement in writing changed? What shifts in writing behaviors do you see? Are notebooks starting to fill?

 # Next Steps

Next Steps for Struggling or Reluctant Writers

By six weeks in, it's quite rare that students haven't produced any writing at all. Reluctant writers might have only a few hundred words, but that is a lot more words than zero. Some of your reluctant writers may have latched onto retelling a popular ghost story, folk tale, or fairy tale or the plot of a game/book/movie they liked. Retelling by writing down words is still a skill. Don't force creativity and the task of generating new ideas on these writers. It is hard to get the right words on a page to help a reader visualize what an ogre looks like, for instance. So that's where you nudge. "If I'd never seen the movie Shrek, how would you describe that character?" Within the retelling context, gently push on character and setting descriptions. Writers build and paint but with words. Another way I go about this is to ask, "But what if your Nana doesn't know what a Charizard (from Pokémon) is or what it can do? How would you write that down for her?" In these conferences, you might also be taking dictation in the student's notebook and then handing that over for them to work with on their own.

Next Steps for Gifted Writers

This trio of genres hits at the emotional engagement center of the brain and some of your gifted writers will embrace that with every drop of intensity they have. Other gifted writers will find getting emotions to the page a significant challenge. What can happen is that they're seeing and feeling the emotion of the scene, but the words to elicit those responses in the reader aren't there. Proceed with care and caution in these conferences. Intellectual endeavor is often a much safer space than emotional endeavor for gifted people. You might shift focus to a mentor text and talk about the procedure of how the writer of the mentor text got the reader to feel thrilled or terrified or laugh, rather than ask a more personal question along the lines of "what do you do when you're scared?"

By now, if not sooner, your gifted writers will have asked if every day can be Free Write Friday. Some of them will be overwhelmed with not only how many words they've written but how many stories they've started. Other gifted writers will have hyper-focused on their favorite genre and been writing steadily on a piece of long form fiction. Since that day (whatever day it was) they've been ignoring the new mini-lessons and writing to please themselves. Honestly, that's the danger of starting with fantasy given how popular it is. The nudge for your gifted writers is to remind them that the overall objective of this work is to grow their skill set across many genres of writing. Encourage them to at least take a few notes and try out a few of the ideas in each new genre, just in case. Also, genres can be blended, and they might pick up some tropes to play with in their piece of long form fiction.

Sports, Historical, and Realistic Contemporary

Sports fiction, historical fiction, and realistic fiction fit together because they all have a strong link to narrative non-fiction and non-fiction writing. Students who are not sure they want to write fiction at all may feel most comfortable with one of these three genres.

We've all taught the student whose main interest is **sports** – usually some combination of watching, memorizing facts, and competing. I developed the sports fiction lesson plans in response to one particular student, but also on a hunch that middle grade and young adult readers might be hungry for that content. Sports fiction, like the other genres we've been studying, has unique tropes and characteristics that form patterns for student writers to follow. For students not interested in reading/writing about battles and fights, sport fiction is a great place to learn about writing action sequences and pacing. Sports fiction also offers a prime opportunity to write ensemble casts and figure out how to write dialog for a group. Not all people follow sports, however. The students who don't care about sports at all might not want to give this genre a try. Remind them that Quidditch is a sport right in the middle of a fantasy novel. Also remind them that each week of genre fiction is both practice and the chance to try something new. (Incidentally trying something new is a great sports trope.)

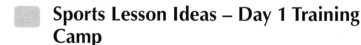

Sports Lesson Ideas – Day 1 Training Camp

The internet is full of sports photos. You won't go wrong using recent images from your hometown team(s) on your opening slide. Sports fiction is physical. Find images that tell a story with body language and facial expressions, like an injured player on crutches leaning forward to watch the game, or a single competitor standing apart from a group, or a coach berating an individual.

Warm-Up

Three story ideas to post:

- She'd never scored so many points before and the game was only half over.
- "Get out there and win. Or don't bother coming home tonight."
- Winning the championship for his hometown was both the best and the worst thing that had ever happened to Wesley.

Invite students to use a combination of the photos and the story ideas to begin their writing for the day.

Overview and Mini-Lesson

More than any other genre, the tropes of sports fiction come from true stories. For my sports fiction slides, I use catch phrases from popular sports shows like College Game Day on ESPN.

Sports Fiction – Keys to the Game

- Write about a sport you know and love.
- If you don't know any sports well, pick the one you're most familiar with.
- Jot a list of the vocabulary specific to that sport.

What? Yes, this is a stealthy vocabulary lesson.

For example, football terms include – Kickoff, Quarterback, Statue of Liberty play, End Zone, False Start, Jet Sweep, Field Goal, Touch Down, etc. You might want to do this as charts or collaborative docs and invite all your various athletes to share their expertise. Depending on the location of the school and community, fewer students might have access to rugby and lacrosse and more students have access to soccer, aka fútbol. For what it's worth, competitive dance is considered a sport and you may have some students who want to write about it. Some students may bring up NASCAR and poker, but since those are for adult competitors only, they're not a great fit for writing about at school. [That being said if you have a student who seems interested in writing for the first time and they want to write about NASCAR, *say yes*.]

If you want to stretch the vocabulary moment just a touch further, ask about terms like "offsides" that many sports use (including hockey, soccer, football, and volleyball) and ask student athletes to explain the nuances of differences between hockey and football or soccer and volleyball in what "offsides" means and the penalties for being offsides.

Remember back when we were studying humor? Sports is a genre where in-group knowledge is critical. The fish-out-of-water/dumb puppet trope works here when a character has zero understanding of the sport and needs an expert to explain to them (as well as the audience).

Sports Fiction – Players

- **Main character** – has to be an athlete (at least in middle grade and young adult sports fiction).
- **Antagonist** – coach, another athlete, teammate, parent, etc.
- **Supporting characters** – any variety, but at least a few should also be on the team, at practices and games, etc.

Questions to think about for the main character:

Are they a superstar? Do they get along with team and coach(es)? Did character choose to play this sport? If so, why? Or is character pushed into competing?

Sports Fiction Tropes

On this slide I use the movie poster for *The Blind Side* (Hancock, John Lee, director. Alcon Entertainment/Warner Bros. Pictures, 2009), but you might want to showcase a great sports novel like *The Crossover* by Kwame Alexander (HMH Books for Young Readers, 2014). Invite students to think of books and movies that use these tropes. Most of their examples will be movies because the sports shelf in most bookstores and libraries is relatively small. Table 5.1, at the end of this section, contains a list of mentor texts for sports fiction.

- The Big Game
- Career-ending Injury
- Accidental Athlete
- Academic Athlete
- Down to the last play
- Ordered to cheat
- Sports hero backstory
- Underdogs never lose
- Ragtag bunch of misfits
- Post-game retaliation
- Huddle shot
- Training montage
- David vs. Goliath
- Based on a true story

For the last ten minutes of class invite students to continue thinking of examples and jotting ideas of sports stories they might want to try. Some students might choose to go home and look up sports vocabulary so they can write a more realistic [insert sport name here] story.

Sports Fiction Day 2 – Getting into the Rough with Characters and Conflict

Warm-Up

Start with photos of current famous athletes from your local or from nationally known teams. If you can, pair these with photos of these people as children. Display the following openers:

- Write about the three biggest obstacles this person faced growing up.

- What rituals or superstitions (like a pair of lucky shorts) does this player have and why?

- Is it better to be the only person in the family playing a sport or is it better if the whole family plays/is involved?

- Is it better to have natural ability or an amazing coach?

Mini-Lesson

Character work in sports fiction shares many similarities with character work in other genres. But sports fiction requires more specifics in certain areas like physique (as it relates to the sport), daily schedule – specific to training, relationships with team mates who may or may not be friends, etc.

Have students choose the character they want to write about and then post Figure 5.1 on the screen:

I used to teach GMC (Goal Motivation Conflict) using *Shrek* as an example, but I think it's even more obvious with sports fiction or something that includes sports fiction tropes like *High School Musical* (Ortega, Kenny,

Goal		Motivation		Conflict	
Internal	External	Internal	External	Internal	External

Figure 5.1 Goal, motivation, and conflict blank

Goal		Motivation		Conflict	
Internal	External	Internal	External	Internal	External
To try something new, like singing, and stay on top in basketball as well	To win the basketball championship	Make sure everyone still likes him, including Gabriella	To fulfill the expectations of his dad/the coach and his teammates	Can a 'jock' also sing and dance? Is impressing a girl more important than the opinions of family and friends?	School expectations and peer pressure dictate that Troy should "get his head in the game" and "stick to the status quo"

Figure 5.2 Goal, motivation, and conflict example

director. Buena Vista Television, 2006). Figure 5.2 is how I would show this for Troy Bolton in *High School Musical*. You can show this to your students but it's probably better to create your own example with something more recent/relevant.

Character: Troy Bolton in *High School Musical*

Once students have played with the GMC for their main characters, invite them to go back to the character interview questions from Chapter 2 and add some details that make this character unique.

Conflict in sports fiction always has more than one layer. Yes, the obvious obstacles and conflicts will be directly related to the sport during practices, games, training, and so forth. But what about having to choose between going to practice and caring for a sick parent? What about sticking with a winning team and a cruel coach versus playing for a mediocre team with amazing teammates and a wise coach?

Once students have completed the GMC table for their main character and added some character details, invite them to try one of the following scenes:

- Five minutes before the game is about to begin and the team captain, also the leading scorer, hasn't showed up.

- The team is behind with only a few minutes left to play and [your character] finds out college scouts are in the stands.

- An athlete who competes against themselves (a swimmer, runner, gymnast, diver, archer) for a better score/time reaches their goal but still loses the competition.

- A character's team is down and they go back in, despite being injured with a potentially career-ending injury.

Sports Fiction Day 3: Color Commentary – Balancing Information and Action

Warm-Up

1. Post a recent sports headline for a less common sport, like curling, or show a short video clip of sports reporting for that sport. Video archives from the Olympic Games are always a great resource for this. Ask students to either jot down questions if they have no idea what's going on OR if they do know all the rules of curling, have them jot down what a non-curling player would need to know to understand the headline/video clip.

2. Now choose a common sport most of your students will be familiar with, at least tangentially, like basketball. Show 45–60 seconds of action from a recent or important game. Have half the class watch and the other half close their eyes. Don't use the audio. The task is for students who just watched to describe what they just saw. Have them write down a few notes and then describe the action to their partner who had closed eyes. Show the clip to the whole class and talk about the challenges of capturing fluid, dynamic movement with words. The students who had closed eyes will want a turn, so use a different clip and repeat the exercise.

3. Finally, if either clip had good color commentary, have the whole class close their eyes and just listen to the professional sports announcer talk about Wisconsin's miracle buzzer beater, or whatever the clip shows. Debrief together about what needs to be included and what doesn't need to be included to give a reader a picture of the action in their mind. Action in real time is different than action being reported on afterward. A sports novel is different than a piece of non-fiction about a team or a specific game. You may have to call this out or show a different example, so students don't accidentally go down the sports reporting path.

117

Mini-Lesson

Earlier in the week, students picked a sport they wanted to write about and today's work is writing an action sequence that balances the information needed (equipment, specific vocabulary to the sport, people in the scene, rules of the game) with the action and emotion of the scene. Just like a fight scene in other genres, an action sequence in a sports story should develop the characters and the conflict, moving the story forward. But because some sports have a complicated structure of rules, positions, equipment, and vocabulary, getting these scenes right requires practice, e.g. reps.

Mentor texts should help with this and will offer lots of options for students to consider like, does the competition have an announcer to give information the main character wouldn't otherwise know? How much interiority (character thoughts) makes sense in certain kinds of action scenes? What techniques speed up or slow down the action and why would a writer choose either of those?

[If you're good with video and video editing, it would be awesome to make a training montage of your students progressing as writers. They're definitely much better at silent sustained writing than they were a few weeks ago!]

Table 5.1 Mentor Texts Sports

Sports	Type of Book	Title	Author
	Picture Book	*Wilma Unlimited: How Wilma Rudolph Became the World's Fastest Woman*	Kathleen Krull
	Early Reader	*Kick, Pass, and Run*	Leonard Kessler
	Early Reader	*Don't Throw it to Mo!*	David A. Adler
	Middle Grade	*The Crossover*	Kwame Alexander
*Historical	Middle Grade	*Step up to the Plate, Maria Singh*	Uma Krishnaswami
	Middle Grade	*Ghost*	Jason Reynolds
*Narrative non-fiction	Young Adult	*Undefeated: Jim Thorpe and the Carlisle Indian School Football Team*	Steve Sheinkin
	Young Adult	*After the Shot Drops*	Randy Ribay
*Graphic novel	Young Adult	*Check, Please! Book 1: #Hockey*	Ngozi Ukazu

Lesson Ideas – Historical Fiction

Historical fiction is more often a favorite of teachers than of students. Teachers like it because historical fiction provides an alternative way to deliver social studies content. School book rooms and classroom libraries often have a fair amount of historical fiction, although many texts have publication dates that are decades old. Older works of historical fiction can be used as mentor texts for today's writers, but the mentor texts listed at the end of this section in Table 5.2 match the style, pacing, and character development more aligned to what current student readers prefer. All that being said, historical fiction offers one thing no other genre has with such abundance, pre-written plot and pre-developed characters. Beginning writers can lean on what history has already said about George Washington Carver, for example, if they chose to write a fictional story about a key moment in his life.

 # Historical Fiction – Day 1

Warm-Up

Open with photographs or images of famous paintings depicting historical figures or events. Try for a mix of ancient, like the Vikings, and relatively recent history, like opening day at EPCOT center in 1982. (In case you're wondering, about 50 years is the over/under on when an era becomes eligible for historical fiction. Stories set in the 70's and 80's definitely have a historical feel, but we're not sure the 90's are long enough ago. Yet.)

Ask students to describe the setting they see using all five senses. Next, even if people aren't in the image, ask them to write down and describe the sorts of people who might be in this moment, in this place. After you complete the sharing routine, ask students to go back and add more detail to the sense of smell to their descriptions. Smell is often overlooked in setting work, in general, but it's critically important for realism in historical fiction. Why? Because ventilation and hygiene practices have changed how the world smells in many places. Smells trigger memories – for example, opening day at EPCOT in 1982 probably smelled like hairspray

119

and cigarettes. Plus, kids like talking about smells and other people's lack of bathing.

Mini-Lesson – Choosing a Topic

Project a world map and divide the class into groups by region or continent, depending on the age of your students. Working in their groups, have students brainstorm lists of famous people and historic events from those regions. After groups share out, invite additional ideas from the whole group. Someone might be an expert in West African history who was assigned to the Australia group, for example. Students should jot down four to five people or events that interest them as they're listening.

Ask students to star or highlight their favorites and then move down a few lines to jot a list of what they might need to know in order to write historical fiction about that person or event. You might ask students to dig just a bit deeper into the topic they want to write about. Perhaps this could be *optional* homework.

Writing from a specific perspective in historical fiction is the equivalent to world-building in fantasy.

Choose a moment in time to model the impact of perspective in historical fiction. For example, in 1900 nearly 20% of American workers were under the age of 16. "Children were ideal employees because they could be paid less, were often of smaller stature so they could attend to more minute tasks and were less likely to organize and strike against their pitiable working conditions." (https://www.history.com/topics/industrial-revolution/child-labor). Children earning money for their families had a different perspective than their parents, educators, adult workers, and labor reformers trying to pass laws to protect children from harmful environments, like mines and factories.

Use an image from this time of children working and use a random assignment technique to divide your class into the above groups (child workers, parents of those child workers, adult workers in the same industry, educators, and labor reformers). Ask them to write about the image, BUT from the perspective they've been assigned. If this is too nebulous, have students jot the pro's and con's of child labor as though they were a labor reformer, a child worker, etc.

Many parts of history have been taught and written about from one dominant perspective. Writers of historical fiction can choose to continue that perspective, or they can choose to write from a lesser known perspective. This gets difficult very quickly, so as your students are brainstorming and digging into their topics, be ready to consult and coach. Where I've seen historical fiction go wrong is when students are not thinking like historians but rather like time travelers, bringing their modern sensibilities to the era/individual in question. If your class is really struggling with perspective, you might have everyone write historical fiction as though they were time travelers. *George Washington's Socks* by Elvira Woodruff (Scholastic, 1991) is a good example of how to do this. For older students, you could use the short story *"Fire Watch"* by Connie Willis as a mentor text. "Fire Watch" was first published in *Isaac Asimov's Science Fiction Magazine* in February,1982 but is available online and in several collections.

In historical fiction, a writer can diverge, at least a little, from the recorded facts. In narrative non-fiction or technical writing, the facts cannot be altered. Some facts seem straightforward, but encompass a lot of information – such as, Sandra Day O'Connor was the first woman appointed to the U.S. Supreme Court. The how and the why of her appointment, the backstory, as fiction writers say, makes for an interesting story. If a student were to choose this topic, "I want to write about Sandra Day O'Connor," you would need to help them filter down to a few key moments, usually obstacles, in her life. Readers and writers are most curious about what a key figure in history had to overcome. The writing challenge lies in crafting scenes around those obstacle moments and piecing them together into a story.

Some historical events are so massive and so much has already been written about them that it's very difficult to narrow down to a few key individuals and a few key moments. For example, I've had students say they want to write about World War II. And when I say that's too large a topic, they say, "Okay, I want to write about the bombing of Pearl Harbor." Even a single battle is still too huge for the purposes of exploring writing historical fiction for the first time. One of my students was able to narrow her interest in WWII down to the day Auschwitz was liberated by Soviet Forces. She chose the perspective of a single solider and ended up with a great piece of writing.

A way to avoid so much variance is to limit the range of topic choices. Some teachers have students research people and moments adjacent to their current class novel, like *The Great Gatsby* or *Esperanza Rising* or *Seabiscuit*. When students research and then write their own historical fiction about the era that they need to understand anyway, it's a win-win. Also, this allows the teacher to curate a set of topics and use that predetermined set to differentiate for student needs. Variation is more fun to grade, but a limited topic range is easier to teach.

Fitzgerald, F Scott. *The Great Gatsby*. Charles Scribner's Sons, 1925.

Ryan, Pam Muñoz. *Esperanza Rising*. Scholastic Inc., 2000.

Hillenbrand, Laura. *Seabiscuit: An American Legend*. Random House, 1999.

Historical Fiction Day 2 – How to Choose a Moment or a Timeline

Warm-Up

Choose a few photographs or paintings that show people in action. The first part of the writing task is to pick one image and then write three things that happened before this moment and three things that happened directly afterward. Plot answers the question, what happened?

Don't share ideas yet. Instead ask students to choose one of the six things they listed and expand it into a short scene using dialog and the five senses to bring the reader into the story. (Yup, that's review, but don't call it out.) After the sharing out routine, debrief about how this worked or didn't work for students. Writing historical fiction is playing pretend about real people and real events. Some of your students will definitely be more comfortable with that concept than others.

Mini-Lesson – The Plot Sifter

Yesterday students chose topics and then did a little research.

Today students need to begin narrowing their topics into something small enough to fit into a handful of scenes.

Plot sifter questions for writing about a *historical figure*:

- Was this time in the historical figure's life a point of conflict AND did the conflict impact later successes? (If not, keep looking.)

- Was this time a turning point in this person's life? What was at stake? What would history have lost if this person had made a different choice? (If not much was at stake, keep looking.)

- Who presented a significant support or significant obstacle in this person's life? Do one or more moments stand out when this support or obstacle impacted the historical figure's contributions or potential contributions?

Plot sifter questions for writing about a *historical event*:

- Can this event be viewed through a single person's experience?

- Did this event take place over multiple days/weeks/months? If so, which single days had the most impact? Could the story of a single impactful day within this event show the historical significance of the event?

- At which points were leaders or key figures making decisions and/ or were people acting on decisions? If the decision had significant conflict before it was reached, this might be a great place to start writing.

You might use George Washington Carver's life as a way to model sifting through an entire history to find the nuggets of significant story. In the late 1890s, George Washing Carver was invited to the Tuskegee Institute in Alabama by Booker T. Washington. Those years had many challenges but also breakthroughs for Carver. Bullet out a few of these and then show a model scene such as Carver having to defend needing a dedicated space for his plant samples. When other professors only had one room, Carver had two. Nearly 30 years later, Carver testified in front of a US. Congressional committee about the importance of tariffs for legumes, specifically peanuts. His testimony was based in his pioneering work with crop rotation; he'd persuaded cotton farmers and they were seeing incredible results. Lay out three to five moments when George Washington Carver had to persuade others about his investigations and the benefits of his breakthroughs. Take one and expand it into a demo scene for the class.

After students have narrowed down their topics, they should have a list of three to five, no more than seven, important moments. They should start turning these into scenes. Good news? The characters are established, as is the setting, and the plot. They get to fill in the conversation and the action with their imaginations. For students who get stuck here, have them jot a list of everything history says about this person. Were they kind? Impatient? Shy? Did they stutter or make grand gestures when speaking? Also have them jot a quick list of adjectives about the setting. Was it cold? Noisy? Crowded? The research and the choices before starting writing take a little longer with historical fiction, but after that, it's similar to writing any other piece of fiction.

Historical Fiction Day 3 – Accuracy vs. Storytelling

Warm-Up

Today's warm-up is a little bit of role-playing. Half the class will be reporters, the other half will be novelists. Post a photo of a recent event, something local and positive, like the opening of a new stadium. The reporter group should work together in pairs and trios to craft a very plain, facts-forward set of sentences about this event. The novelist group should work together to craft flowery character and setting-forward sets of sentences about the event. Your students probably won't know the phrase "purple prose" but you might. This is what the novelist group is trying to write, gooey over-written purple prose. If you tell them to "add lots of drama," they will probably know what that means. The novelist group may include as many or as few of the facts as suits the narrative they're crafting. They can also embellish on the information – not to the point of adding dinosaurs rampaging, but they might add adorable kittens or kindly grandmothers if they wish. Depending on the size of your class, you'll have several of these masterpieces from each group and students who want to read aloud/perform them for the class.

 ## *Mini-Lesson*

After the silliness has settled, explain that historical fiction has to split the difference between these two extremes. Historical fiction tells an interesting story at least loosely based on facts. Draw a continuum like this:

Technical writing...Narrative Nonfiction...Historical Fiction.
No story – just information...Story and Information...Mostly story-some information

Facts can be blended into setting and character descriptions.

> *The guys joke that a submarine is just a tin can with a motor. And they're right, except for the part where if anything breaches the tin can, you'll die.*

> "His wooden teeth clacked shut as a fresh idea popped into his mind."

Facts can slide into dialog.

> "It's five in the morning, why is the house shaking? My god, the whole street is shaking!"

If students began writing scenes yesterday, they should examine the scenes for how many facts have been incorporated so far. An average of three-five facts per page is about right, some pages might have fewer. Since this is historical fiction, no page should have more than ten facts or the writer is just info-dumping.

What Is an Info Dump?

"An info dump is an extended form of telling (rather than showing). An info dump is a big chunk of information that is 'dumped' in the reader's lap all at once. These info dumps are usually done through narration but can be found in dialog as well." ellenbrockediting.com

Example of what not to do:

"The creature chased her into the ancient castle at the top of the hill. Local historians claimed it had stood over a thousand years. In the summer the castle hosted a very popular renaissance festival and in the fall it hosted an equally popular Oktoberfest. Angelica tripped on the weathered marble steps as she ran deeper into the entryway. She was pretty sure the tour guide had said all castles in Rhineland, including this one, had secret passageways. Maybe she could find one on her own?"

Why not? – it is unrealistic that a character being chased by a monster would be thinking of the history of the place where she is being chased. The second part, hoping to find a secret passage is a better, smoother way to do this.

Another example of what not to do:

"As you know Hugh, Formula One racing is the highest class of international single seater auto racing but it came from the European Grand Prix in the twenties and thirties."

Why not? – "As you know" is often in the *Top Ten Mistakes* writers make with dialog. If a character is telling another character what they both know, it rings false. If the writer is trying to get a date in there, a character might say, "We've been the best since the thirties, eh Hugh?" Or something that acknowledges both characters know the information and conveys the information but in a more natural way.

You might want to stop and practice different ways to incorporate facts and/or you might want to spend some time highlighting how facts are incorporated smoothly in the mentor texts. Some students are much more natural at this than others. And some students will be so in love with the facts they've uncovered that they want to jam them into the story at the cost of narrative flow. When I'm teaching this, I admit to my students that loving facts and research is the main reason why I haven't had a lot of success writing historical fiction. Once I heard a writer speak about a novel in which the original Paris opera house was a key location. She said she researched it for days, but in the end only three pieces of information, one as small as the type of wood used for the trim on the balcony, made it into the book.

Anachronism is another pitfall for writers of historical fiction. Like most Midwestern students, I learned this word while being taught Shakespeare's *Julius Caesar* in which a clock strikes. Our teacher explained that although Shakespeare had clocks, the Romans did not. Anachronism is a fun word to know. This is something you would share as a quick reminder during the drafting phase, but potentially add to an editing checklist for historical fiction later.

Students should use any remaining class time to continue practicing integrating information into the story and adding words to their historical fiction draft.

Table 5.2 Mentor Texts Historical Fiction

Historical Fiction	Type of Book	Title	Author
	Picture book	Dancing Hands: How Teresa Carreño Played the Piano for President Lincoln	Margarita Engle
	Picture book	The Power of Her Pen: The Story of Groundbreaking Journalist Ethel L. Payne	Lesa Cline-Ransome
	Picture book	Schomburg: The Man Who Built a Library	Carole Boston Weatherford
	Early reader	Maritcha: A Nineteenth-Century American Girl	Tonya Bolden
*Historical science fiction	Middle grade	When You Reach Me	Rebecca Stead
*Historical fantasy	Middle grade	Dactyl Hill Squad	Daniel José Older
	Middle grade	One Crazy Summer	Rita Williams-Garcia
	Young adult	Code Name Verity	Elizabeth E. Wein

Lesson Ideas – Realistic Contemporary Fiction

Every class has at least a few students who love to read and write **realistic fiction**. Sometimes these stories lean toward romance, but more often they're stories about friendship, moving, bullies, difficult adults, and other relatable topics. Realistic fiction tends to skew a little sweet and idealized for middle grade readers and gritty and dark for young adult readers. It's very important to revisit the four rules for writers' workshop before you spend a week with realistic fiction. Despite your best efforts, exemplars might hit too close to home for some of your students.

Realistic Contemporary Fiction Day 1

Overview

Begin with brief definitions of realistic and contemporary. You might turn this into a game of "what it is and what it isn't" or you might have a stack of ten books with half being from other genres and half being realistic, contemporary fiction and see if the class can help you find the right ones. Prior to embarking on this genre study, realistic contemporary fiction would've probably been called "books." At this point, however, you and your students know that fiction is sorted into categories and each category has its own writing patterns. The reason to start with definitions is because if you don't, and you put up some photos for writing warm-up, some students will add a mystery or magic or something else that doesn't fit in this genre. You will likely be clarifying this "what it is and what it isn't" for the whole week. The mentor texts listed in Table 5.3, at the end of this section, may help with this clarification.

Warm-Up

Show a handful of photos of people doing general, everyday sorts of things – relative to your community. Simply ask students to describe what they see, with a focus on the people. [I once worked for a boss from San Diego.

Watching regattas was a fun activity for his family when he was growing up. Whereas, I am from Nebraska and we have no ocean, so no regattas whatsoever. If you are teaching this in Nebraska, no regatta photos for you. If you are teaching this in San Diego, no tractor photos for you.] For this week, the focus *is* on Write What You Know which means keeping everything within students' typical experiences. One of the best parts of this work is seeing the people and places you always see from a new perspective.

After you complete the sharing routine for the warm-up, explain that contemporary realistic fiction doesn't have tropes in the same way other genres do, but it does have patterns that must be followed for a story to be included in this category.

The basic guidelines are the following:

- The characters are engaging and relatable.
- The dialog sounds like everyday people (of this time) talking, relative to the setting.
- The setting is either a real place or a place that is just like a real place.
- The problems faced by the characters are *current* problems in the world.
- The resolution makes sense.

Mini-Lesson – Developing Characters for Contemporary Realistic Fiction

Real people must be crafted and brought to life on the page with the same attention to detail as science fiction clones and fantasy elves.

Whereas in previous genres it's been fine to be flexible about age of characters and age of audience, for this genre, students will be designing main characters who are +/– 3 years within their own age and creating stories that are for readers who are also roughly their age. While this genre might need a little research when it comes to the setting, for the characters, the writing power comes in already knowing.

Sketching with Words

Select a photo you haven't used yet of a person who looks like your students. If you can, find a photo of a person doing something, like eating ice cream or sliding into home plate. Together describe the details of the person's appearance. Revise as you go. Does the person in the photo have big eyes? Long lashes? Do they have high-arched eyebrows that make them look perpetually surprised? Do they always have at least one scab on their knees? Your students will want to start with easy stuff but push for specifics. The specifics will feel like too many words for when a character walks onto the page for the first time. But it's better to have too many words than really boring everyday words like tall/short, young/old.

Students won't have a photograph of the character they're going to write about. They will need to close their eyes and imagine a photograph of that person and then start writing following the same progression in describing appearance that you just modeled. Some of your students will have a name for this character already. But if they don't, forbid them from worrying about names. Why? If you don't, they will waste *hours* researching names and origins of names. And they won't have written anything. Since they're "sketching" they should be working through this person's appearance first and then filling in the background in the imaginary photograph.

After you and the class are satisfied with what you've written so far to describe the main character's appearance, ask a few other questions like, does anything make this character's appearance unique? What would another character, meeting this one for the first time, notice? With older students you might ask, what is an assumption that others make about this character, based on their appearance, that isn't true?

The next layer of character work is about who the character is as a person. First question, does this person's insides match their outside? Some real-life people look nice and sweet and kind and are truly terrible human beings. Some real-life people might look a little rough on the outside but are smart and honorable in everything they do. From there, have students list personality traits and characteristics that define their soon-to-be main character. Go back to the photo you described together as a class and practice, if needed. Is that person friendly? Funny? A sore loser? Someone who struggles to read? Someone who always shares the dessert in their lunch? Personality traits can be a single word: Mean. They can also be a phrase: most likely to cheat if the ref wasn't looking.

Invite the class to go back to their main character and add some words or phrases to describe this individual's personality and how they act in the world.

The last layer of this activity is to continue mining for connections and contradictions between the external and the internal. Does this person look like a big tough high school basketball player and yet, they melt at the sight of a puppy or a kitten? Does this person look like a stylish, all-pulled-together valedictorian and yet they apprentice in an auto-detailing shop after school, wearing coveralls and getting greasy? While every character embellishment needs to stay in the realm of the believable, encourage students to have fun with this. Also, encourage students to sprinkle in some contradictory traits. No human is all business or no party.

With luck, this work opens up a handful of plot ideas, including some that could carry the story students are about to write.

Day 2 – Settings in Realistic Contemporary Fiction

Warm-Up

Post a picture of your school building. Ask students to note how old they were and how long ago they first entered this place. Then they should jot lists of what they noticed on their very first day. Depending on the age and transiency of the population, you will have students who started in the school years ago and some who are rather new. Just like with describing the appearance of main characters yesterday, push for more specific details when possible. My favorite question to ask: *Where is the best water fountain in this school?* I've yet to have a group with no opinion. The best water fountain is sometimes "coldest" and sometimes "tastes better."

 ## *Mini-Lesson*

Setting is world-building and world-building flows from point of view. How the character notices the setting doesn't just show the spaces they are moving through, it also develops what the reader knows about the character as a person.

Ask students to skip down a few lines and write some ideas about how the main character they worked on yesterday would see your school.

Would they notice all the exits? Would they be relieved the building had air conditioning? Would they count how many other kids looked like them?

List the three to five key places where scenes in this person's (the main character they worked on yesterday) story will take place. Examples might be:

- School – cafeteria, classroom, hallway
- Home – bedroom, kitchen, bathroom
- Neighborhood – skate park, coffee shop, hangout
- Work – if the character is old enough to have a job
- Church/Synagogue/Mosque – if religion is an important part of the character's life

Once lists are made, writers should highlight the one to two places that are most significant to the character AND where the action will take place. The bulk of today's writing is building out those settings the way the character would see then. Intergalactic assassins as well as ordinary Earth humans have unique points of view. The fun of setting work in contemporary, realistic fiction is bringing a place to life using the specific lens of the main character.

If students aren't sure how to do this, direct them back to the lists of characteristics and personality traits. Someone who loves cars would notice not only the fanciest cars in the neighborhood, but the ones they could fix up if the owner was interested. Someone who loves puppies might hang out at the dog park or try to start a dog-sitting business.

Day 3: Plots in Contemporary Realistic Fiction

Warm-Up

Choose a popular story or a book you've read as a class and summarize the plot in the following format:

Once upon a time _____
And every day _____

Until one day _____
And because of this _____
And because of this _____
Until finally _____
*And ever since that day ___

I often use the animated *Mulan* film as a model. (Cook, Barry and Tony Bancroft, directors. Walt Disney Pictures/Buena Vista Pictures, 1998. Based on *The Ballad of Mulan* by Guo Maoqian.)

> **Once upon a time** *there was a girl named Mulan who lived in a small town in China with her family.*
>
> **And every day** *Mulan did chores and helped her injured father while her family tried to get her to be ready to get married.*
>
> **Until one day** *a messenger from the Emperor came with orders for her father to re-enlist and join the war. But Mulan's father had an injury from the last war and was too weak to fight.*
>
> **And because of this** *Mulan cut her hair, took her father's sword and horse, and went to join the army.*
>
> **And because of this** *Mulan had to hide her identity as a female and rise up to the many training challenges in the army camp.*
>
> **Until finally** *Mulan used her cleverness and bravery to save the Emperor.*
>
> **And ever since that day** *Mulan's family was proud of her and her legend lives on in China.*
>
> *Adapted from McDonald, Brian. Invisible Ink: A Practical Guide to Creating Stories That Resonate. Talking Drum, LLC, 2017.*

Mini-Lesson

Draw a flow chart (or flow map) that shows how problems flow from character. At the beginning of a story characters already have problems, but while they might solve some, they always get or cause more problems. By taking on her father's identity, Mulan solves the problem that he might be hurt or killed in the war. But she creates new problems by having to hide that she is female.

Settings also begin with problems and during the course of a story the setting may add more problems. Weather conditions and traveling long distances either marching or on horseback are setting-related plot problems in Mulan.

Ask students to jot down three character problems and at least one, but as many as three, setting problems their main characters might have.

If students are feeling a little stuck, you might offer ideas from one of the following lists, depending on the age of your class.

Possible Plots in Realistic Contemporary Fiction

Grades 3–6 Real-life problems, elevated:

- Moving/new kid
- Bullies
- Lonely/Isolated
- Divorce
- School is too hard/easy
- Irresponsible or unreliable parents

Grades 7–8 Hidden or less-talked-about real-life problems:

- Homelessness/hunger
- Drug or alcohol use/addiction
- Intense prejudice/targeted bullying
- Death/dying

Once students have some ideas about problems the characters might encounter, they're ready to plug them into the stems, Once Upon a Time, etc. The seven stems should be the seven scenes students are now ready to write.

Contemporary, realistic fiction does not use plot tropes for structure the way other genres might. However, the following characteristics tend to be true of this genre:

- Writing usually *emphasizes* and *lingers on* the <u>emotional context</u> of what is happening in the main character's life.
- The story still has to have a beginning, middle, and end.

- The story still has to have stakes that feel intense and impactful to the main character.

- Sometimes the main character changes in significant ways, sometimes not.

- Sometimes the people *around* the main character change.

A good example of this is the 2006 film *Akeelah and the Bee* (Atchison, Doug. Lionsgate Films, 2006). This film follows some sports tropes as well, but ultimately is about Akeelah's journey of discovery about who she is and what she can do.

The key difference in some contemporary, realistic fiction written for upper middle grade and young adult readers is the stakes may actually be life and death. That being said, the boundaries are gray and changing all the time. As students are conferring with you about plot ideas, you will likely need to make student-by-student decisions about appropriate content. And even more than during the study of other genres, be ready to check in with the mental health team. Students' writing may be more personal and reveal previously unknown needs and concerns.

Recipe for Realistic Contemporary Fiction

- Start with a compelling character.

- Show that character's everyday life.

- Introduce an external challenge or an antagonist or both.

- Show an internal challenge that might prevent the main character from overcoming the external challenge/antagonist.

- The main character tries and fails (at least once, usually more than once).

- The main character makes the internal change that they didn't want to make/didn't know they could make.

- The final time the external challenge/antagonist appears the main character demonstrates how they have changed. They don't always "win," but they've overcome something or learned something important.

Table 5.3 Mentor Texts Realistic Contemporary Fiction

Realistic Contemporary	Type of Book	Title	Author
	Picture book	*Where Are You From?*	Yamile Saied Méndez
	Picture book	*Hair Love*	Matthew A. Cherry
	Early reader	*Juana & Lucas*	Juana Medina
	Middle grade	*The Fresh New Face of Griselda*	Jennifer Torres
	Middle grade	*Marcos Vega Doesn't Speak Spanish*	Pablo Cartaya
	Middle grade	*Gaby Lost and Found*	Angela Cervantes
*Graphic novel	Middle grade	*New Kid*	Jerry Craft
	Young adult	*Color Me In*	Natasha Diaz
*Sci-fi twist	Young adult	*The Grief Keeper*	Alexandra Villasante

Ask Your Students

Ask your students about their experiences with historical and contemporary realistic fiction first. Quite often, these two genres get a lot of airtime during read alouds and book talks. They also tend to occupy a majority of the real estate on classroom library shelves.

Next ask about sports fiction. Find out how much they've read and how much they *might read*, if it was available. Some students will probably have good ideas for mentor texts to use while you're studying sports fiction as a genre.

Ask about why, since sports leagues are so prevalent in many communities as well as college and professional sports being so dominant on television, don't we have a comparable amount of sports fiction in bookstores and libraries? At the end of this genre fiction study, have students draw or make a pie chart of their ideal library, assigning a percentage of shelf space to each type of genre fiction with a total of 100%.

Some of my students' ideal libraries would look like:

75% Fantasy.
10% Humor.

10% Crime.

3% Historical.

2% Realistic Contemporary.

Or

50% Science Fiction

20% Historical Fiction.

15% Crime.

10% Romance.

5% Sports.

Ask Yourself

Is the contemporary realistic fiction in your collection still contemporary? Many of the Newbery Award winners were of their time and would've been considered contemporary when they won but now would read more like historical fiction to students. Would any of the realistic fiction or historical fiction in your classroom be considered fun to read by students? Some teachers tend to over-purchase books that teach historical content and/or books that teach a life lesson. Students may be drawn to historical fiction or contemporary realistic fiction for this exact reason – but when choosing mentor texts for learning to write, storytelling must come first.

Does your bookshelf and your modeled reading represent a balanced diet of all types of fiction and non-fiction? Do you talk with your students about what you're reading in your free time? At one of the middle schools where I worked, every Thursday morning instead of regular homeroom, we had silent reading for 20 minutes. I made a point of bringing in whatever I was actually reading at home. It was important on those days to talk about reading for fun versus reading to learn/reading for school. Students were required to complete two to three choice novels a semester in addition to whatever texts were assigned. Thursdays ended up being a great time for spontaneous book talks and book enthusiasm.

Another thing I did very purposely was collect my favorite sentences and story ideas from my "reading for fun books" in my writing notebook. And I made sure to mention I was doing this either during homeroom or during class or both. This habit has only become more magnified over the years and now I find I'm frequently in "that gives me a story idea" mode.

Then and now, I make sure to have at least a moderately balanced reading diet. I have my go-to genres that are comfort food, but I also force myself (in some cases) to read other genres and non-fiction that isn't related to work. Just like we force ourselves to eat vegetables or tofu to get a little additional nutrition, forcing ourselves to read "healthy" books is good. When our students only see us reading books that are the literary equivalent of a vegan bran muffin. They might think, "if that's what adult reading is like, no thanks."

A balanced writing diet is just as important as a balanced reading diet. Sometimes writing can and should be just for fun. Sometimes writing, either the topic or the process or both, is a challenge to help us grow. If we want our students to become lifelong readers and writers, how we model and the experiences we provide now create that foundation of healthy, sustainable habits.

Next Steps for Gifted Writers

Gifted writers may or may not connect as easily with sports fiction, historical fiction, and contemporary realistic fiction. BUT the gifted students who love baseball or who have a deep interest in trench warfare will love this unit. Gifted writers who want to write these genres will need support not only choosing which information is critical to their fiction, but also *eliminating* the information that isn't necessary in their story.

Of the three, contemporary realistic fiction might be the most challenging for gifted students because it requires the writer to magnify everyday events and emotions – something that might feel even more uncomfortable than writing about romance. If a student gets stuck, invite exploring the idea of the ordinary or every day in a fantasy setting or a crime story. In fantasy stories, siblings still fight, but they might be elf siblings instead of human siblings. In crime fiction, main characters also have families and mundane responsibilities, like washing dishes or taking meals to Grandma. These scenes are critical to making an otherwise unstoppable, highly skilled heroine relatable. The other, more complicated but fun option is to offer a little genre blending, such as historical crime fiction. This might help a gifted writer move through the block and back into drafting.

Next Steps

Next Steps for Struggling or Reluctant Writers

Reluctant writers often love these three genres because they feel familiar both to their own experiences and to the books they've been exposed to at school. Curate a set of sports resources and a set of historical resources ahead of time to eliminate a key frustration for struggling writers – trying to find information and reliable sources. You might print or link the best three articles about top Olympic sprinters for a student you know will choose that topic. Or if you're narrowing down choices to connect with a single class novel, work with your library media specialist to help you find non-fiction books and articles related to *Unbroken* (Hillenbrand, Laura. Penguin Random House, 2010.)

Reluctant writers will also need more time and very specific modeling with mentor texts to navigate how to use information in their sports and historical fiction stories. For these challenges, be as flexible and supportive as possible about any and all attempts. Acknowledge that this is hard, but it can also be both fun to read and write if the topic is intriguing.

Contemporary realistic fiction produced by struggling writers might look a lot like a "slice of life" story or a "bed to bed" story at first. These are both legitimate starting points and probably reflect writing instruction the students' received in prior years. Depending on the individual, you might be happy they completed the assignment and move on. Or, you might have a writing conference where you encourage the writer to find the most important part of the slice of life or single day. The two questions, "what's the most important part?" and "WHY is that the most important part?" lead to a conversation about expanding that important section and also if the student is willing and interested, how to expand it.

Fan Fiction

The Super Sneaky and Extra Fun Way to Prepare for Narrative Assessment Tasks

 Overview

When you spend as much time as I do researching released items from state tests, you start to notice patterns in the narrative writing tasks. For example, 90% of them are based on a text or a video, or both, provided within the testing environment. The types of tasks include "Write an original story using the details you've learned about the characters" and "Continue the story" and "Retell the story from X character's point of view" and so on. In short – fan fiction.

Not all teachers know about fan fiction, but many do. And many more students not only know about it but love it and write it in their free time. Fan Fiction involves close reading/close viewing and getting into the details of the thing you love, whether it's a book, television show, film series, celebrity's life, or manga. In this chapter, you'll find a huge pile of examples and lessons to sneak in practice for the state test in the guise of modeled writing about Captain Marvel's origin story.

While gifted readers are not usually excited about close reading, gifted people are often extreme fans of things, like the Marvel Cinematic Universe (MCU). They understand how critical it is to get the details right and how that might involve re-reading, re-viewing, etc.

Reluctant writers embrace fan fiction because it provides so much structure and support, e.g., writing within the game world of *Animal Crossing: New Horizons* (Nintendo, March 2020) offers an established setting, established characters, and established goals and challenges. They don't need to invent anything, instead, they can focus on getting something on the page. If you are the sort of teacher who doesn't like to do things in order, yes, you could start your writing year with Fan Fiction. Just make sure to revisit it ahead of state testing time.

Fan Fiction Day 1

Warm-Up

Choose images from three popular TV shows or movies
     For younger students, I've used *Sponge Bob*, *Spiderman - Into the Spider-Verse*, and *Frozen II*. For older students, I've used *Stranger Things*, *Black Panther*, and *The Hollow* (cartoon on Netflix)
     It's better to pick three so that students can connect to at least one of the pictures. Students may ask to do one of these prompts about a different show/movie/book. And yay, that's great. Successful fan fiction depends on the writers' love for and knowledge of the thing they're writing fic about.
     Each image gets its own prompt:

- Write a few sentences about what you imagine happened on Sponge Bob's first day in Bikini Bottom.
- Write the worst part of Miles Morales's first day at Brooklyn Visions Academy.
- Write a new ending for *Frozen II*.
- Write a new ending for *Stranger Things* Season 3.
- Tell a part of *Black Panther* from Shuri's point of view.
- Tell a part of *The Hollow* from Kai's point of view.

Hillenburg, Stephen. Season 1, episode 1 *Sponge Bob* "Help Wanted," 1999.

Persichetti, Bob, et al., directors. *Spider-Man: Into the Spider-Verse*. Columbia Pictures/Sony Pictures, 2018.

Buck, Chris and Jennifer Lee, directors. *Frozen II*. Walt Disney Pictures, 2019.

The Duffer Brothers. *Stranger Things*, Season 3, episode Chapter 8: The Battle of Starcourt, Netflix, 2019.

Coogler, Ryan, director. *Black Panther*. Marvel Studios/Walt Disney Studios, 2018.

Mepham, Josh, et al. *The Hollow* Season 1, episode "The Room," Netflix, 2018.

After the sharing routine concludes, ask the group who reads fan fiction. Next, ask who already writes fan fiction. I've yet to work with a group with zero fanfic writers. But teachers are sometimes surprised by who responds yes to this question. More often than not the current fanfic writers in the group will say something along the lines of "yeah well it's not like writing for school" or "I didn't think you would like it because it's not real writing" or "my fic writing is personal and I don't talk about it at school." In fact, I know teachers who write fanfic in their free time and didn't think it was real writing either!

Mini-Lesson

A quick internet search will result in some fun images with the words Fan Fiction or Fanfic. Post one of these along with the definition:

> **Fan fiction or fanfiction** (also abbreviated to fan fic, fanfic) *is fiction about characters or settings from an original work of fiction, created by fans of that work rather than by its creator.*
>
> **Fan fiction** is defined by being both related to its subject's canonical fictional universe (often referred to as "canon") and simultaneously existing outside it. Most fan fiction writers assume that their work is read primarily by other fans, and therefore presume that their readers have knowledge of the canon universe (created by a professional writer) in which their works are based.

I usually include a separate slide with a photo of an actual cannon and the question, "What is the canon exactly?" The answer: Canon is the original story. This means anything related to the original source including the plot, settings, and character developments.

Before moving on, ask if anyone has both read *The Lightning Thief* by Rick Riordan (Miramax Books/Hyperion Books for Children, 2005) and seen the film adaptation of *Percy Jackson and The Lightning Thief* (Columbus, Chris, director. 20th Century Fox, 2010). Ask the students who raised their hands, "And what part of the book's canon was changed by the film?" Fans of the Percy Jackson books get incensed about the movie, so be ready. The first answer is usually about Annabeth and how she looks in the book (small, blond hair, gray eyes) is not how she looks in the film (tall, muscular, red hair). Give other examples of canon characters and settings that can't be changed. Younger students will likely have seen *The Lorax* film (Renaud, Chris, director. The Illumination Entertainment/Universal Pictures, 2012) or the most recent *Grinch Who Stole Christmas* film (Mosier, Scott and Yarrow Cheney, directors. *Dr. Seuss's The Grinch*. Universal Pictures, 2018). These also alter the characters and plots of the original books and could be considered to have violated canon.

Open the website An Archive of Our Own (https://archiveofourown. org/). This is the most current and largest fan-fiction site. As of this writing it hosts writing from nearly 40,000 fandoms across categories such as films, books, TV, comics, real people, bands, anime, cartoons, etc. Say, "this website has 40,000 fandoms. Please list your personal top ten." I often follow-up with something like, "If I said you would have to write fan fiction for an assignment, what fandom would you choose? Camp Half Blood? Magic Tree House? Supernatural?" Some students read/write fanfiction about real-life You Tube stars and some read/write about popular bands. For this week's purposes, that is all fine, as long as the original property and the writing are okay for school.

Osborne, Mary Pope, and Sal Murdocca. *Magic Tree House*. Random House, 1998.

Singer, Robert, and McG. *Supernatural*. created by Eric Kripke, season 5, episode "Swan Song," 2010.

Trouble shooting: *Occasionally, I have students bring up canon content that isn't okay for school, like the* Die Hard *franchise (McTiernan, John, director. Twentieth Century Fox, 1988). How I handle that is to have a one-on-one conference with the student about what kinds of scenes they could write (Jon McClean playing with his kids, attending a neighborhood BBQ) that would include the most important character but keep the content age-appropriate. Of course, you could just say no. But as luck would have it, the students asking about super scary horror movies or truly violent action thrillers are often the ones who haven't engaged with writing much and I want to find a way to say yes and get them writing.*

Today's writing is to try "what happened right before" or "what happened right after" scenes.

Choose a clip from another familiar property, like *Avatar: The Last Airbender* or the reboots of either *Voltron* or *She-ra and the Princesses of Power*. For older students, you could use any of those or *The Mandalorian* or *Brooklyn 99*. It doesn't matter which series you choose, just pick an action or battle scene that lasts 2–3 minutes.

Ehasz, Aaron. *Avatar: The Last Airbender*. created by Michael Dante DiMartino, and Bryan Konietzko, season 1, episode "Chapter 2: The Avatar Returns," Nickelodean Animation Studios, 2005.

Hendrick, Tim. *Voltron: Legendary Defender*. Season 1, episode 1–3 "The Rise of Voltron," Dreamworks Animation Television/Netflix, 2016.

Stephenson, Noelle. *She-Ra and the Princesses of Power*, Netflix, Nov. 2018.

Favreau, Jon. *The Mandalorian*. created by Jon Favreau, season 1, episode "Chapter 2: The Child," Lucasfilm/Disney Media, 2019.

Del Tredici, Luke. *Brooklyn 99*. created by Dan Goor, and Michael Schur, season 1, episode "48 Hours," Fox/NBC, 2013.

After watching the clip, invite students to write the scene that happened right before this one or the scene that happened right after this one.

- What typically happens **before** a battle: gearing up, discussing the plan, checking on team members.
- What typically happens **after** a battle: bandaging injuries, celebrations, grief, anger, cleaning and storing weapons.

Sometimes the show or film skips over these types of scenes for the sake of time. But fans love to think about their favorites either doing or not doing hero-worthy activities.

An example of an unpredictable post-battle scene is in the end credits of the first Avengers film (Feige, Kevin. *The Avengers*. Marvel Studios/Walt

Disney Studios, 2012). Fans of the MCU love the tiny little clips that show up during and after the credits. In this one, the main characters are all eating shawarma. During the battle, Tony Stark had quipped that he's never had shawarma and it's kind of a throwaway line. This scene is the payoff of that line.

If students aren't ready to think about battles and action, use the picture book *Miss Nelson is Missing* by James Marshall (Scholastic, 1991). Review the story together (or enjoy reading it together) and then ask, "What happened when Miss Nelson got home after her first day as The Swamp?" Brainstorm some ideas together, like, she made herself dinner and took a long soothing bath. She cried. She laughed. She threw her Viola Swamp wig on the floor. And use those ideas to write a few sentences about what happened next.

Some students might want to go back to the fic of the thing they love and/or go back to the fic they started during warm-ups and add a scene. And again, great!

Fan Fiction Day 2

Warm-Up

Write about a setting from another point of view.

Rather than use a specific canon text/film, use a photo or illustration of a mildly spooky-looking forest. Then list several of the standard fairy tale characters one might find in and around such a forest: young child, witch, wolf, prince/princess, fairy, hunter. Each of these characters would have a different point of view about walking through the forest.

Invite the class to choose a character and write a few sentences about how they see the spooky forest. For example, a wolf might want to stay hidden so it would be happy about shadows and low-hanging branches. A young child might be nervous about every sound and stay on the path OR a young child might be distracted and curious and wander off the path immediately.

The most common reasons a character would have a unique point of view about a setting are that character has secrets/backstory reasons and the character's job, goal, or role affects how they see the setting at that moment. A knight who has spent years in battle would always be looking at defenses of structures or how to protect the people they're escorting, for example.

 ## *Mini-Lesson*

After completing the sharing routine for warm-up, show an image of the book *Wicked: The Life and Times of the Wicked Witch of the West* by Gregory Maguire (Regan Books, 1995) next to an image of the Broadway poster for the musical *Wicked* (Schwartz, Stephen and Holzman, Winnie 2003) and ask if any of the students have heard of *Wicked*. Next, ask students to guess how much money has been made on this wildly popular piece of fan fiction. (You might also have to ask, "What was the canon text for *Wicked*?") Check the numbers, but at this writing, it's close to a billion dollars of revenue between the books, Broadway and touring company ticket sales, and merchandise.

For those who have read *The Wonderful Wizard of Oz* by L. Frank Baum (George M. Hill Company, 1900), the pleasure of *Wicked* is viewing the characters in a new light and learning "the untold story" of the Wicked Witch of the West.

Next show an image of the four DC character backstory novels, called the DC Icon series, written by popular YA writers:

- *Wonder Woman: Warbringer* by Leigh Bardugo (Random House Books for Young Readers 2017).
- *Catwoman: Soulstealer* by Sarah J. Maas (Random House Books for Young Readers 2018).
- *Batman: Nightwalker* by Marie Lu (Random House Books for Young Readers 2018).
- *Superman: Dawnbreaker* by Matt de la Peña (Random House Books for Young Readers 2019).

One of the things to practice today is interiority or character thoughts. Ask students, haven't you ever wondered what Catwoman thinks about when she's planning a heist? Or how does Batman psych himself up for a fight? Many comics are told from a third-person point of view, so character's thoughts and feelings don't make it to the page like they might in other types of stories.

For older students, another great mentor text is *X-Files Origins: Agent of Chaos* by Kami Garcia (Imprint, 2017). This is a YA novel set during Fox Mulder's senior year of high school where he investigates a series of disappearances similar to his sister's disappearance. (If you have older students who want to write a thriller, this is the mentor text to give them.)

For younger students, read together or revisit *The True Story of the 3 Little Pigs!* by Jon Scieszcka and Lane Smith (Puffin Books, 1996). This book is such a great example of both backstory and looking at events from a different, in this case, the villain's point of view.

Two video clips that work well for this lesson:

- The tragic backstory of Dr. Heinz Doofenschmirtz from the Disney cartoon *Phineas and Ferb* is hilarious but gets the point across about how he became a villain. (Povenmire, Dan and Zac Moncrief, directors. Season 1, Episode 46 "Unfair Science Fair," Disney Channel, 2009.)
- In the *Lego Batman Movie* (McKay, Chris, director. DC Entertainment/Warner Brothers Pictues, 2017), Batman has a scene with Alfred in which Alfred reminds him of all the things Batman has been through since his parents died. Alfred gently scolds Batman for pushing people away.

Today's writing is about fan fiction that develops backstory. After so many fun examples, students will be ready to write. Many may want to continue with characters from the fic they started yesterday. Others may be more intrigued ·by villains now and want to play with those ideas. For students who are feeling stuck, offer the option of a common fairy tale retell from the villain's point of view. Or, simply to draw, list, or write the backstory for a well-known Disney villain like Scar in the animated film, *The Lion King*. (Allers, Roger and Rob Minkoff, directors. Walt Disney Pictures/Buena Vista Pictures, 1994).

Advanced Variation of Backstory or Untold Story – 'Shipping

'Shipping is the practice of putting two characters in a relationship that is not canon. Writers often talk about their own work, like "X and X" are a canon couple, but feel free to 'ship everyone else. Fic writers 'ship canon characters too but in the community, they have to tag the piece as a non-canon 'ship so fans and readers who are curious about Hermione and Draco's secret relationship, for example, know they've found what they're looking for.

Fan Fiction Day 3 – Scenes to Try and the Connection to State Testing

Warm-Up

The cartoon series *The Hollow* (Mepham, Josh, et al., episode 1 "The Room," Netflix, 2018) offers a fun take on the idea of getting to play inside your favorite video game. Show the opening few minutes of season 1, episode 1. Today's prompt: *imagine you won the chance to experience your favorite (book/game/show/movie) as a new character. The catch is that you will have amnesia when you arrive in that world. Describe how you feel when you first wake up, what you notice, who helps you or doesn't, and your first task.*

I started teaching Fan Fiction because my older daughter came home and reported how much fun she had writing fanfic for the state test. Aghast, I ran for the released item's webpage and discovered, yup, all those prompts could be considered fanfic by an experienced fanfic writer like my child.

Mini-Lesson

At the beginning of this chapter, I talked about all the released items I've read from various state tests.

Here are some examples:

4th Grade

Today you will read the story "There's Plenty of Fish in the Trees" from Ivan: Stories of Old Russia. As you read, pay close attention

to point of view and the events as you answer the questions to prepare to write a narrative story.

- What would the story be like if it were told from the wife's point
  of view?
- Consider how descriptions and events might change based on the
  point of view of the person telling the story.
- Retell the story from the wife's point of view. Include specific details
  about the setting and events that occur in the story to support this
  point of view. (PARCC 4th Grade ELA - Released item 2017)

6th Grade

In the passage from *Zoobreak* [by Gordan Korman], the author
develops two very different characters named Ben and Griffin.
Consider the details the author uses to develop these two
characters.

- Write an original story that continues where the passage ends.
- In your story, be sure to use what you have learned about the
  characters as you tell what happens next. (6th Grade PARCC ELA
  2018 - Released Item)

8th Grade

Today you will watch the video *Hanna's Gold*. As you watch, pay
close attention to the characters and plot as you answer the
questions to prepare to write a story.

You have watched a video in which the main character, Hanna,
makes a mysterious discovery. Think about the plot of the video
and think about how the characters react to the events that occur.

- Extend the events in the video by writing a story that describes
  what happens next.
- Be sure to include details from the video in your story. (8th Grade
  PARCC ELA 2018 - Released Item)

The most common narrative tasks for state tests include the following:

- Retell the story from a different character's PoV.
- Extend the story by writing the next scene/a new scene.
- Write a NEW story using the characters, setting, etc.

- Write a prequel or backstory that sets up the character relationships, situation, introduces the setting/problem, etc.

- Write an alternative ending.

- Write a journal entry from a specific character's PoV about the events **in** the excerpt, events **that preceded** the excerpt, **or** events that happened **after** the excerpt.

While it is completely understandable that many Literacy blocks and Language Arts classrooms spend more writing minutes on expository and persuasive writing, narrative tools are not only necessary (and part of standards) but tested in many U.S. states.

Some state tests show videos for the writing prompt, some use excerpts from short stories, plays, or novels. But the tasks listed above are common across most sets of released items.

As you're showing these examples don't let them ruin the fun of fanfic! Fan fiction is a legitimate and growing genre in and of itself. And, it just so happens to be the most fun part of the state test.

Today's Writing

Students can continue any of the fanfic pieces started this week. Or they might try one of the types of story starters often found on state tests that they haven't tried yet. Or, knowing what they know now they can start a full fic from scratch.

The Fanfic Recipe

- Pick an established world, set of characters, etc.
- Generate a list of stories that haven't been told (that you know of – Star Wars universe is hard!).
  - Be thoughtful about where this story would fit in the established timeline.
  - Be mindful of your audience, e.g., rabid fans.
- Draw a picture or make a list of what is "canon" for that world, set of characters, etc.
- Start writing.
- Have fun!

The following fanfiction example is considered "pre-canon" but is also "canon compliant" and was written for fans of the *Xenoblade Chronicles* games (Developed by Monolith Soft for Nintendo, 2010–2020).

Pre-canon Xenoblade Chronicles Fan Fiction

From "Little Snowdrop" by Simone E.

> Prince Kallian was nervous.
>
> The feeling was unfamiliar, rarely encountered within picturesque Alcamoth. Usually, given any suddenly unsteady beats of the heart, all it would take was a glance up at the wide expanse of blue sky or more often the bright and distant stars to recover some sense of purpose and stability. Many of the High Entia had a tendency toward being nearly nocturnal, Kallian was no exception. He wasn't as aggressive an astronomer as some of the Alcamoth residents, but it was hard not to become entranced with the colors that draped the far off points of light, seemingly painted with some heavenly sponge brush. But it wasn't night now, and the uneasiness persisted.
>
> Melia fixed her half-brother with a glare far too large for her tiny body, hands balled into fists around the skirt of her dress. But she waited between the symmetrical trees nonetheless.
>
> Kallian nervously clasped his hands behind his back, then quickly decided against the motion and in an equally nervous manner clasped his hands in front of him. "Good afternoon, Melia!" he said, unsure of if he should attempt to close the distance between them.
>
> "And a good afternoon to you as well!" Melia's response was in equal measure polite and indignant, and with it came a huff of finality. She stomped off into the gardens around the villa.
>
> Clearly leaving the half-siblings unsupervised like this was by design, so Kallian followed after Melia into the garden. She was sitting among the flowers and grass in a place that seemed to have been flattened for this express purpose. Kallian made his way over slowly, making certain he didn't accidentally step on one of the many blooms.
>
> For a while the air was stiff with silence. Kallian was uncertain of whether it was the grass or lack of conversation that was more uncomfortable, searching desperately for something worthwhile to say.
>
> "Are you... Enjoying your studies?" he asked, finally. But the regret was instant with the realization he'd done nothing but parrot a line from their father.
>
> Melia had clearly come to the same conclusion, letting out another huff. "Do you not remember?"
>
> Kallian frowned. "Remember what?"

"My answer from when you last asked. And last visited."

Kallain attempted, somewhat unsuccessfully, to minimize his outward expression of embarrassment. "My apologies."

Another stretch of silence, but this time it was Melia who broke it. "If you had asked if perhaps my answer had changed since then…"

"Ah!" Kallian could tell he was being thrown a line, and it would have been an injustice to Melia not to take it. "Is there– has your answer changed?"

She nodded, pleased. "Yes. I have been greatly enjoying botany."

"Botany?"

"For the sake of this garden, you see." Melia gestured to the flowers, which swayed gently as she did.

"It is a lovely garden. Clearly your efforts have not gone to waste."

Melia gave him the same look he assumed she might if he had been describing in graphic detail the digestive system of a slug.

"You've no reason for such confidence." Melia scowled, which was an expression that did not entirely match the rest of her relatively downy personage.

Kallian had no reason to be dishonest with her. "Father speaks highly of your progress in all of your studies, Melia."

"Does he?" the scoff was apparent in her words, "If he truly has such faith in my abilities, one would assume that he would allow me some greater freedom."

"What sort of freedom do you mean?"

Melia took a deep breath. "I would like to go outside."

Kallian frowned. "Outside? I am happy to accompany you anywhere in Alcamoth, given the proper permission."

"No!" Melia threw herself backward onto the grass. "Not Alcamoth. I want to go truly outside. See the Eryth Sea, the Syrath Lighthouse… all of it." She closed her eyes, all the better to imagine the scenery. "Surely, it is even more beautiful than the textbooks describe?"

Kallian looked up at the sky, uncertain of how to answer. He had no intention of lying to Melia, but worried at the consequences of confirming her fantasies. That, and he was not entirely disposed to long outdoor excursions. "It is beautiful," he said, "but I am not certain the scenery would live up to your expectations."

Melia sighed. "I know you only say that because of the supposed safety risk. If Father truly had any such faith in me, I do not think I would be left to imagining."

"There is more at stake than your safety, Melia. It has nothing to do with your talents."

She sat up, fixing Kallian with a stare that he immediately knew he didn't like. "Prove it, then. If you believe in me so blindly, take me outside."

Kallian stiffened. "I cannot possibly—"

"I do not mean right this instant," Melia was quick to clarify, noticing his distress.

"I..." Kallian took a deep breath, for composure's sake. "I am not entirely certain there is anything written that expressly prohibits you going outside. If you are truly set on doing this, I will make the arrangements."

Melia's eyes sparkled with surprise and excitement, the sudden emotion reflected in an inadvertent flap of the wings on her head. "You would do that for me?"

"Consider it a token of apology."

"For what?"

Kallian smiled, a little ruefully. "Always asking you the same question, among other things."

A voice called out for the two of them in the direction of the villa gate. Kallian stood, followed by Melia. By the trees where he had entered stood the Second Consort and the soon to be Emperor, Melia's mother waving to get their attention. He made as if to leave, but she tugged on his sleeve, beckoning him down to her height.

"What you said is a promise, yes?" Melia whispered conspiratorially once he had leaned down.

"Yes," Kallian agreed, attempting to match her volume, "It is a promise."

Melia let go of his sleeve with a pleased half-nod, then skipped off to join her mother by the trees, somehow avoiding every flower in the garden on her way. Kallian again found himself among his father's procession, crossing the long bridge back to the central palace.

Sudden motion caught his eye as they progressed, and he turned around. Melia stood, in the same place as before, but not at all the same position. She had one arm up, jauntily waving goodbye. After a moment of consideration, Kallian returned the gesture.

And he wondered if perhaps there had been no reason to be nervous in the first place.

Ask Your Students

Ask your students if they ever watched a show, saw a movie, or read a book that "got it wrong." Meaning the ending wasn't satisfying or a really important subplot wasn't resolved, or the wrong characters ended up together. Most of them will say yes.

Observe who gets really into fan fiction and who doesn't. Keep offering options and remind students and yourself to stay open to the possibilities.

As you're conferring this week, definitely check in with students about how it feels to write in someone else's story world. Many of them may notice that they've been incorporating elements of their favorite shows or characters in their other types of genre fiction.

Ask Yourself

Veteran teachers all have those moments we flashback to with a wince, thinking, "If only I'd known then what I know now…" One of mine is from my first year of teaching and is with a student who was often a grumpy, non-participator. In the memory, it's writing time and he wants to write new scenes with the two main characters from his favorite show. Brand-new-teacher me says, "No, you need to use your imagination and create something new." Ugh. Head smack. He would've been creating something new and more importantly, he would've finally written *something*.

I had a chance to "fix" this a few years ago with a 4th-grade student who passionately declared how much he hated writing the first day we met. He only liked Math and Pokémon. Veteran me said that he could write about Pokémon every day if he wanted. And guess what? The student who never wrote produced seven short pieces of Pokémon fanfic over the course of a month.

Did that mean this student was ready to write a standard essay? No. But the experience gave him feelings of success during writing, a feeling that supported him at least trying other types of writing the remainder of the year.

Elaboration is one of the four dimensions of creativity measured by the Torrance Test of Creative Thinking. And elaboration on someone else's creation is at the heart of fan fiction. Thinking up an entire cast of characters, setting, and plot on your own, especially for a beginning writer, can feel impossible. Writing a scene in an established world, with established characters is like bowling with the bumpers on. New writers just have a better chance of hitting the pins with supports in place.

If you already read and write fan fiction, do you have any fics you could share with students? Can you talk with them about the community of fans and writers and the connections shared through mutual love of (the thing you write about)? I've written *X-Files* (Created by Chris Carter, Fox,

1993) fan fiction and *Supernatural* (Singer, Robert, and McG. created by Eric Kripke) fan fiction and it was so fun. Those pieces aren't great writing examples, but I experienced a lot of joy and satisfaction in writing them.

If you've never read or written fan fiction, did you consider *Wicked* (Schwartz, Stephen and Holzman, Winnie 2003) to be fan fiction?

Could you make time in the cycle of your writing year for fan fiction? Would you be willing to try fan fiction yourself?

Next Steps for Gifted Writers

Some gifted writers jump in and love fan fiction with all the enthusiasm they already had for their fandom. The opportunity to connect with a community of fans can create happiness and ease the sense of isolation gifted students sometimes have. Don't be concerned that a student's particular love won't have a fan base and fan fics already written. Some fandoms might take a bit more digging to find, but they're out there.

On the other hand, some gifted writers will feel like writing fan fiction is stealing or copyright infringement. For those students, you might need to walk through the fine print of Archive of Our Own (https://archiveofourown. org) and some of the language around fair use, commercial use, etc.

Most gifted readers have opinions about books and what the writer needs to do next with the series. For the ones worried about copying, point them toward writing new fics "set in the world of." In those sorts of fics they can keep the canon characters or create new characters for that world. Gifted writers taking on that challenge will also likely attempt to match the style and tone of the series. Any time a student writer is getting down to the most important writing question, which is "how did they do that?" they are well-positioned to grow in their own craft and writing skills.

 # Next Steps

Next Steps for Struggling or Reluctant Writers

The option to write in an established world using established characters (and sometimes plots) is an excellent scaffold for reluctant writers. Using these scaffolds, reluctant writers can let go of the burden of imagining everything new and practice on the other areas of writing craft like dialog and action and bringing people and places alive on the page.

Fan fiction has also supported my students acquiring English by providing choice and storytelling support. Sometimes, I listen and scribe as emerging bilingual students tell me about their favorite animé or favorite You Tuber and the story ideas they have. Making a connection between something the writer loves and the ideas they have about it is often a magic "ah-ha" moment for students who would otherwise say they can't write or hate writing.

One year I had an emerging bilingual student who loved Minecraft (Mojang Studios, Microsoft Studios, 2011) in my creative writing elective. Minecraft has a main character named Steve who builds things and searches for items to use in crafting and creating. To be honest, I often have students who love Minecraft, but this one wanted to live inside the game. For the first several weeks of class, the student wouldn't write, so during a conference I asked him what he loved and would he be willing to write about that. For the rest of the quarter, he wrote every single day adding to his Minecraft story. Better yet, other Minecraft lovers in the class would ask him about the story. "Did Steve get any sheep?" "Did Steve find enough red stone?" So not only was this student now writing, he had positive reinforcement from the community. And because he wrote every day, he ended up with a relatively long piece of writing, and his skills increased as well.

Based on a True Story
Narrative Nonfiction

Overview

Rumors and sales trends hint that narrative nonfiction is a fast-growing segment for both the middle grade and young adult markets. To my thinking, that trend has roots in a lot of places, including students' need for "the truth." Narrative nonfiction is an easy step away from fiction because it still uses plot, character, setting, and dialog. Instead of telling an imaginary story, you're now using your narrative toolbox to tell a true story. Best case scenario, while creating narrative nonfiction, student writers discover that writing can be a tool for thinking and learning.

"Why not start here?"

Great question. That word nonfiction feels comfortable and safe to many teachers. Nonfiction is something teachers might already have lesson plans and templates for. BUT in order to earn student writers' trust, you must first provide time, space, and tools to write what they love to read the very most – Fantasy, Crime, and Humor. AND narrative nonfiction is a lot harder to create, and less fun, without a complete road-tested toolbox of fiction writing tools. When you get here, mid-late second quarter, student writers will have more confidence and more buy-in for the act of writing.

The genre fiction templates in this book have been honed and refined over many, many groups of students from 3rd to 8th graders. As much as I love genre fiction and would write/teach only that, I knew my students and the standards required more. With less experience but a strong desire to offer narrative nonfiction to my students, I started with mentor texts. Students may have experience with reading nonfiction, but less than half of what might be in anthologies and the school library would be considered *narrative* nonfiction.

The following definition comes from the Masterclass website:

> "The genre of narrative nonfiction requires heavy research, thorough exploration, and an aim to entertain while also sharing a true, compelling story. Narrative nonfiction, also known as creative nonfiction or literary nonfiction, is a true story written in the style of a fiction novel. The narrative nonfiction genre contains factual prose that is written in a compelling way—facts told as a story. While the emphasis is on the storytelling itself, narrative nonfiction must remain as accurate to the truth as possible." (https://www.masterclass.com/articles/understanding-narrative-nonfiction)

As you prepare for narrative nonfiction, spend a week during *reading* time offering robust, age-appropriate pieces of narrative nonfiction text. What you'll notice is that a larger-than-average swath of what is currently published in online/print magazines like *National Geographic* and *Smithsonian* falls along the narrative nonfiction lines. As you read examples together, be sure to highlight the narrative tools in use. You'll typically find figurative language, lively verbs, rich descriptions of people and places, and more often than not, some dialog.

The Notice It, Name It, Try It (in Chapter 10) protocol works really well here. For example, after reading a short piece of narrative nonfiction about how llamas have unique antibodies, direct students to find an example of figurative language such as the one in this article from the *Today* show (NBC News, 2020) "A virus is like a piece of Velcro and antibodies attach to that Velcro to prevent it from attaching to our cells." (https://www.today.com/video/how-llamas-are-helping-create-antibody-treatment-for-coronavirus-86334533852) As a group you notice this sentence, you name it "This is an example of a simile" and then you invite students to try their own simile. Simile is an excellent tool that brings something unknown or less well known, like antibodies, closer to the reader's understanding by comparing the unknown thing to a known thing, in this case, Velcro. How you try this technique is up to you and depends on the students in front of you. You might have them write a new simile to explain how antibodies work. Or if that's too challenging, have them write a simile about something they've learned recently in science or history. Offer several choices. During your week of reading narrative nonfiction exemplars, be sure to notice, name, and try as many narrative tools as possible. You might add discussion or thinking homework questions like, "what did the writer do that worked overall in this piece of writing?" And, "how is this different from textbook nonfiction?"

Unlike the genre fiction lessons, the narrative nonfiction work will take longer than a week. Three weeks should be about right, depending on how often you see your students. Instead of breaking these plans into three days, they will be broken into Week 1, Week 2, and Week 3 activities. Depending on the time of year and other schedule impacts, this might roll into a 4th week. Do your best to keep it within that time frame or writing enthusiasm and engagement may falter.

Narrative Nonfiction Week 1: Research Like a Writer/Generate Ideas

Warm-Up

Post three sets of facts without pictures – only 2–3 sentences each
    I use:

* The "Miracle on Ice" – U.S. Olympic Hockey story.
* Dr. Mae Jemison – first black female astronaut.
* He Jiankui – created first genetically altered babies.

The prompt is: *Choose one of these sets of facts to write about for your warm-up today.*

After the sharing routine ask, "What is the difference between an **interesting** true story and a **boring** true story?" Have students jot down their thinking.

Mini-Lesson

Show a picture and the map/timeline of the Thailand Cave Rescue. Students may or may not remember this from 2018, but it was a riveting story with several real-life plot twists. Ask, "What are some of your favorite true stories?" As students are jotting those down, also ask, "Why are those your favorites?" Students will bring up the Titanic, 9/11, the U.S. Women's Soccer win at the Olympics, among others.

Next have students start a list called: Things I Would Research if I Had Time.

Write your own list and be ready to share it. Here's mine:

- Astronaut training
- Competitive riflery
- True hauntings
- Neuroscience as it relates to quantum mechanics
- Field medicine
- Radio astronomy
- Roswell crash
- FBI recruitment practices
- Prion diseases
- Drought-resistant gardening for food
- Carlsbad Caverns

Send students to their desks/devices and ask them to research the people who go with those topics if they haven't listed people as topics. For example, Ruby Payne Scott was a pioneer in Radio Astronomy, so I could use her story as the lens through which I write about radio astronomy. If they listed people, have them note the thing the person is known for, like Dr. Mae Jemison is known for being the first Black female astronaut.

Choosing a topic for your first narrative nonfiction piece of writing can be complicated. You need the Goldilocks topic that's not too big or too small, the amount of available information has to be just right. Here's a simile – writers are like crows and magpies, we collect shiny, unusual, interesting bits of ideas. As you and your students dive into research, attend to the shiny, attractive bits of learning, but make sure everyone is vetting internet sources and can put together a small pile of **facts**. If only a few facts are available, such as conspiracy theories about Denver International Airport, encourage students to save that idea for another day and keep looking. Two possible mini-lessons on these first few days: a) how to know if your topic has the "just right" amount of information for narrative non-fiction and b) facts and evidence versus theories

I use a model lesson on my topic of choice, the alleged Roswell crash and coverup. I talk about how I was inspired by *Project Blue Book,* a show on the History Channel, which is narrative nonfiction based on over 12,000 declassified U.S. Air Force case files and investigations of UFO's. (O'Leary, David. *Project Blue Book.* Season 2, "The Roswell Incident" Parts 1-2, History, 2020.) Each episode of the show focuses on a single incident which is a just right amount of information. Between the books, articles, websites, movies, and shows, the information about Roswell is too much, so I narrowed my topic down to why people think the U.S. government covered up the crash in Roswell, New Mexico in 1946 of an unidentified flying object. Just as with genre fiction, you must do this work alongside your students. Otherwise, you won't have firsthand experience of the obstacles and the rewards. As mentioned previously, this is critical to having authentic writing conferences, especially during this unit.

Unlike previous weeks, writing minutes are sacrificed for research minutes. Research is a writerly activity. However, writing a little every day is always a good idea. Have students write similes and metaphors about their top choice topic on one day and write dialog about that topic on a different day. Students might also collect lists of vocabulary words associated with the topic(s) under consideration. The sacrifice of writing minutes allows you to spend more time in short bursts of conferring about topic choices and helping students with research. Specifically, try to confer with each student about their topics by the end of class on Friday of Week 1.

By the end of Week 1, students should have chosen a topic and collected a pile of facts, roughly 15–25 pieces of information, and shared these (with links to their sources) with you. Don't skip Free Write Friday! Everyone needs a break from research and the opportunity to shift back into creative mode. Here's a basic guideline for the narrative nonfiction product.

	# of Facts	Total Word Count	Time Frame	Works Cited
4th Grade	8–10	300–600	3–4 weeks	Yes
7th Grade	10–15	600–1200	3–4 weeks	Yes
9th Grade	15–20	1200–1500	3–4 weeks	Yes

Figure 7.1 Narrative nonfiction product guidelines

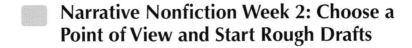

Narrative Nonfiction Week 2: Choose a Point of View and Start Rough Drafts

Warm-Up

Post pictures of three different doors. Look for images that are wildly different, like a Hobbit door, the massive door of an elephant enclosure, and the door to a bowling alley.

Label them plot, setting, and character in whatever order feels appropriate to the pictures.

The prompt is: *which door is more inviting to readers and why?*

Alternate prompt: *Pick a door and describe what's behind it.*

For example – *I think an abandoned Chuck E. Cheese is behind the setting door. The tables are dusty and the animatronic band is frozen mid-song. The skee-ball lanes are empty and darker spots on the concrete floor mark where thin carpet runners and some of the games used to be.*

After the sharing routine, talk for a few minutes about how plot, character, and setting are the three doors into narrative nonfiction, and choosing the right door for their topics is a key goal of this week.

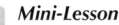

Mini-Lesson

Into Thin Air by Jon Krakauer (Villard, 1997) is a narrative nonfiction that uses the setting, Mount Everest, as the vehicle for the story. *Hidden Figures* by Margot Lee Shetterly (William Morrow, 2016) uses the perspectives of three African American women at NASA to unspool the story. Character is the primary doorway of Hidden Figures. Plot is the doorway for books like *Black Hawk Down* by Mark Bowden (Atlantic Monthly Press, 1999) and *In the Heart of the Sea* by Nathaniel Philbrick (Penguin Books, 1999). In reading these two books, people learn what truly happened, but through riveting storytelling.

Post excerpts from the beginnings of each of these books and notice how the author uses the doorway to focus the experience of the reader.

While modeling, I share how I chose plot as my doorway. I wanted to write a piece of narrative nonfiction that helped readers understand *what happened* in 1946 and has happened since to keep the Roswell conspiracies alive. Ask students to think about and then make notes for which doorway (plot, character, or setting) their topic lends itself to. They might want to try an opening sentence of two to see if the doorway works.

Alternative mini-lesson texts for younger students:

Claudette Colvin: Twice Toward Justice by Phillip Hoose (character) Farrar, Straus, and Giroux 2009.

Lincoln's Grave Robbers by Steve Sheinkin (plot) Scholastic, 2012.

Where is Area 51? By Paula K. Manzanero (setting) Penguin Random House 2018

I Survived: Hurricane Katrina, 2005 by Lauren Tarshis (plot/setting) Scholastic 2011

Top Secret Files: Pirates and Buried Treasure by Stephanie Bearce (character) Prufrock Press 2015

*series of titles that would be useful for narrative nonfiction mentor texts

Mini-Lesson – Balancing Facts with Narrative Tools

Any given paragraph shouldn't have more than 3–5 facts. A paragraph that reads like a list of facts is not narrative nonfiction. A paragraph that reads like a textbook is also not narrative nonfiction. Choose a dry, factual paragraph on an otherwise interesting topic, like the Bermuda Triangle, to rewrite together. Students will definitely need to practice this with you.

Example 1 – post the opening paragraph from Wikipedia (or a similar source) about the Bermuda Triangle. It is full of facts and vocabulary. It is informative, but not necessarily engaging.

Show a few examples of travel articles about Bermuda, and the main tourism page for Bermuda and then choose parts from both Wikipedia and the travel articles to incorporate into an opening paragraph.

This won't go very smoothly at first. Some students will think the Wikipedia article is great and others will prefer the travel articles. Narrative nonfiction has to be both informative and interesting.

This week students might spend time rearranging their pile of facts into smaller, more specific piles, e.g., eyewitness accounts, statements issued to the press, conflicting statements from equally credible sources. One of my students did a lovely piece of narrative nonfiction about red pandas. Her piles of facts included: habitat facts, misconceptions about red pandas, current risks to red pandas' survival, and current efforts to sustain populations of red pandas. These piles of facts will lend themselves to paragraphs or sections of the narrative nonfiction piece.

You might have additional, invitation-based mini-lessons to refresh setting tools, character tools, and plot tools. Any student could attend any mini-lesson, but they must attend the mini-lesson specific to the doorway they've chosen. During these mini-lessons, students will be practicing alongside you to apply these tools to their groups of facts.

All this time without laying down a lot of words on the page might feel strange to you and your students. You've built so much stamina together. Students will be extra ready to begin rough drafts this week, but make sure they've got the following before they begin: a *just right* topic, a pile of facts sorted into smaller piles, and a doorway/perspective to use for the story. Extra conferences probably need to happen this week as well. I think nonfiction feels different, more like school, and therefore more like something that will be graded. I also think students have such a limited frame of reference for narrative nonfiction that they need more support than in previous weeks.

Of course, students can and should work on their drafts during Free Write Friday. But if they need a break to return to their stories about centaurs robbing banks, let them.

 Narrative Nonfiction Week 3: Finishing Drafts, More Mentor Texts, Peer Editing, and Final Revisions

Warm-Up

Post pictures of three recognizable places in your community – they might be special occasion places, like a professional sports stadium, or everyday places, like a hardware store.

Prompt: *Tell a true story about this place, or a story that* could *be true, based on what you know.*

Mini-Lesson – Using the Rubric to Assess Progress

Professional writing is governed by word count because all publishing is digital. When introducing this project, you gave students the final word count range and the scoring rubric. I recommend using a version of the Analytic Writing Continuum from the National Writing Project which can be found in the book, *Assessing Writing, Teaching Writers: Putting the Analytic Writing Continuum to Work in Your Classroom* by Mary Ann Smith and Sherry Seale Swain (Teachers College Press, 2017).

Take a short section of one of the mentor texts and compare it against the rubric. Make sure to choose something of similar length to what your students are producing. Next have students take one paragraph of their current draft and use the rubric to analyze how close they are to their desired outcome. Practice using the language of the rubric to talk about the text. "I notice this section has dialog and that brings the scene to life."

Mini-Lesson – Revisiting Peer Conferences with Narrative Nonfiction

Prior to turning students loose to give feedback to one another, invite a student or another teacher to join you in a model conference. Go over the rules before you begin. The model conference should last no more than five minutes (explain that their conferences will be longer because they will need time to read). After the model conference, debrief with the whole group what they noticed. Collect and chart sample questions writers might want feedback about at this point in their process.

Sometimes teachers only want students with complete drafts to engage in peer feedback. Given the challenges in the project, please consider allowing those with only partial drafts to participate as well.

Narrative Nonfiction Peer Feedback Routine

1. Writers jot down a few questions they need feedback about, for example, "is the dialog working?" Or "would another simile be helpful in this section?"

2. Working in pairs, writers exchange writing, and requests for specific feedback. They can use sections of the rubric to target their requests.

3. At the end of the conference, each writer will state what they will add or change in their drafts.

4. At the end of the conference, each writer will thank their partner.

Rules for This Routine

- Use the language of the rubric to guide your conversation.

- All comments must be specific to the writing, not the writer. "I noticed this section has eight facts and no narrative tools at all." Versus "You didn't put any narrative tools in here."

- You cannot ask, "Do you like this?" even though that's what you're dying to ask.

- You can ask, what might make this piece of writing work better, read more smoothly, sustain the reader's interest, etc.

- You cannot say something critical like, "This is terrible" or "You should start over."

In order to maximize the feedback received by students, set up at least two rounds of the peer feedback routine.

Along with word count, professional writing is governed by deadlines. The final draft of narrative nonfiction is due at the end of class on Friday or after 15 total class days. Some teachers allow students to work on writing assignments at home, some do not. Before students turn the draft in, have them grade themselves using the rubric. Ask students to highlight sentences or words in their final drafts that demonstrate where in the text they've used lively verbs and excellent figurative language.

Since this is the only long project included in this book, it seemed best to include examples from three different students.

From, "Archery" by Garrison W., 7th Grade

Maybe it's the click of the nock sliding into place. Maybe it's the thwack the bow makes when you fire off the perfect shot or even the thud of carbon arrows against the thick foam. Whatever it is, there is something satisfying when you shoot your bow. A compound, recurve or even longbow, the Olympics are an event you don't want to miss. But how do those skilled shooters get to be where they are?

Getting on the team certainly isn't like your high school tryouts. Your country wants the best athletes they have. A nation receives 3 spots in the men's and women's brackets if they placed in the top 8 in the World Archery Tournament the year before the games. If not, they acquire a grand total of one participant. Three is because there's no I in a team sport (actually because that's how many people on an Archery Team). The team gets a medal each if they place in the top three at the Olympics The competing countries then select certain individuals to participate. Often, these trials continue in the spring of the year of those Olympics. The person or team must meet the standards of World Archery as well.

But how in the world are these amazing individuals so relentless in their training? How do they keep going once they begin that amazing journey? A way anyone can start off is having a game of archery dodgeball. This sport combines two popular activities, dodgeball and archery. "Isn't that a safety hazard?" one might ask. The arrows are launched from a standard recurve bow, built with cheaper materials so as to be both cost efficient and safer. All arrows have a large marshmallow looking pad on the front so that no one gets hurt. Although you can still catch one for the out, I wouldn't recommend it because, well, it is still an arrow....Another way to start is hunting. The archery season always starts earlier

The most common myths keep so many from competing. One is the lie that archery is dangerous. Archery is actually three times safer than golf. It is even one of the world's safest sports, with a single injury per every 2000 participants. Another game stopper is one that says that your eyesight has to be good. This is a complete lie. No other sport lets you wear glasses - any glasses - while going for the gold. Visually impaired Im Dong Hyun is a two time olympic gold medalist, and the record holder for the 70 yard shot. Other completely blind archers may use tactile sighting technology to execute their best shot. One more of these myths less real than any greek myth is that little voice in our heads that says, "Don't I have to get really strong to do that?" Nope. Any company or trainer will start you out on a trainer bow. These are easier to pull back, at a draw weight of 10 pounds. As a result, I wouldn't recommend the 70 yard range. Oh, and that one, "Isn't all that stuff expensive?" It will only be as expensive as you want it to be. And one of the best, "Do I have to wear green?" Thanks for nothing, Robin Hood.

From "Red Pandas" by Clarity N., 7th Grade

"Hey, Yibo, you see anything?" Fuwen said as he looked around solemnly.

"I wish, but no." Yibo kicked a smooth pebble down the path ahead of them. "Our job was hard enough to begin with but if this keeps up we might not ever find enough red pandas."

"Yibo we can't stop now, we're so close! We only need two more specimens!

"We haven't seen two together in months. What makes you think our luck is changing now?"

"It's breeding season. If they weren't together before they should be now. If we're lucky we'll find a female and she can bring the males right to us!" Fuwen cheered with so much confidence it was like hearing a lion roar.

"So what? If the locals continue to do this despite our efforts then it's no use."

"If we find the proof we need then we can work on getting better protections in place. They won't be able to do this anymore, or at least not as easily." He gestured behind them towards the damaged land." Yibo smiled, knowing Fuwen was right. With renewed confidence the group was off. The gentle breeze flowing through their hair and the smell of success carried on the wind

Previously this had been part of the surrounding forest indistinguishable, healthy, and alive. They had even gathered some of their first samples there. Now this land was damaged, empty, and with no trees for food or shelter the animals had disappeared too. Such a travesty further demolished this furry creatures' habitat, already limited and encroached upon. In fact, habitat loss is one of the number one reasons red pandas are endangered.

Paw prints tracked through the soft earth before them and at a glance they could make out leopard tracks and huge panda paws. Droppings, torn up trees, and half chewed branches told them they were on the right track. The scientists weren't looking for leopards or pandas. Not the black and white kind, at least. Their target was a bamboo eater as well, but much smaller and much more colorful than the iconic bears often associated with these forests. Despite this they continued on, for where you find pandas you find red pandas. This is because the much larger giant panda only eats bamboo stalks whereas the smaller, more nimble, red panda only eats the bamboo leaves leading them to coexist in perfect balance.

From, "True Crime: Los Angeles" by Caden E., 7th Grade

It's a beautiful September day, the leaves gaining a slightly orange tinge as the temperature starts to finally cool down...As I finish up my lunch at Nick's Cafe, the scent of hamburgers and cheap coffee trails me all the way to my squad car. I cruise along Santa Monica Boulevard, stopping for a couple of parking tickets on overdue parking meters. I don't get to patrol the streets too often anymore after transferring to Hollywood Detectives, so today is a nice change from reports.

A muffled voice comes over the radio. All I can get from it is "De Longpre Avenue." I head over, since I'm only a couple minutes away. As I pull up, I already see four other squad cars and an ambulance with wailing sirens with an EMT crew. It is setting that this is much more serious than I thought.

I try to remain calm while getting out of my car. When I get to the front door of the studio apartment, I see the most heinous scene of my career. Bright red blood spattered on the entire wall. As I walk in, I see a few other officers searching the entire apartment. When nothing turns up, we head back to the station for further instructions on how we will take care of finding whoever did this. Upon exiting, I see a brutally beaten young girl lying on a stretcher inside an ambulance. While driving back, I can hardly focus on the road as these thoughts and feelings crowd in my head like people at the Walk of Fame.

Upon my return to the station, Lieutenant Jenkins instructs us to not go searching for the perpetrator. I suddenly get filled with rage.

"We need to go out and find who beat that girl! Who knows what they'll do next!"

"I understand that Detective Hodel, but the only description we have is from this man, and he didn't get a very good look," Lt. Jenkins replies as he gestures to a man in all black and a leather jacket. "We don't know enough about this man to just go find someone to arrest." I reluctantly agree, but I still feel like I must do something to find him. I can't let him get away with this like my father did with the Black Dahlia case.

Ask Your Students

Ask your students to reflect on the process of writing narrative nonfiction. Which step or steps was the hardest? Some students struggle to choose a research topic. Some students struggle with adding narrative tools to something that has facts. Another group of students might have strayed into historical fiction rather than sticking to verifiable information in service to writing a better story.

Ask students about the peer editing routine and what worked or didn't work for them. Check in about revision as compared to line editing as well.

As a reflection activity, my co-teacher and I asked the students to write a letter to next year's 7th graders with advice about the narrative nonfiction unit. Many of them revealed more in these letters about how they "wasted" time trying to find the perfect topic, or tracking down unhelpful information than they had shared during class conversation and conferences.

Ask Yourself

Ask yourself where or when in your non-teaching life have you encountered narrative nonfiction? How did that compare to standard nonfiction in terms of how you retained the information? After books, magazine and website articles are probably the most visible products of adult professional writing.

What did you notice about student engagement in narrative nonfiction compared to genre fiction and fan fiction? Are you seeing patterns across different groups and types of students?

 # Next Steps

Next Steps for Struggling or Reluctant Writers

Struggling or reluctant writers may or may not enjoy narrative nonfiction. It's more tangible and more school-like than the previous work on genre fiction. The structure of this project might be comforting to some reluctant writers. But this assignment might feel close enough to the writing they've disliked in previous classes to bring up old, stuck feelings and behaviors. Some of these writers will need smaller increments and smaller word count deadlines during the three weeks. They might need additional trouble shooting on choosing a just right topic. As always, celebrate every written word and every completed section while providing specific praise and feedback whenever possible.

Next Steps for Gifted Writers

Gifted writers will want to exceed the word count limit for this assignment. Don't allow it. Adding more words doesn't necessarily make a piece of writing better. You might dust off your college copy of *Elements of Style* by

Strunk and White (Macmillan, 1988) and show them rule #1 Omit Needless Words. Related to this is the revision challenge many gifted writers face. They don't feel revision is necessary and/or they continue to confuse revision (strengthening the writing) with editing (correcting grammar errors). Others will revise too much, never feeling ready to turn the work in.

The gifted students who love nonfiction may or may not love narrative nonfiction. These will be your students who crave straightforward technical writing which we will get to fairly soon.

Use the Narrative Toolbox to Win Arguments

 Overview

When the Common Core State Standards landed, whether your state adopted them or not, classroom emphasis on nonfiction reading and writing, especially persuasive writing, increased dramatically. Only one chapter of this book is devoted to the art of persuasive writing because schools have been flooded with writing programs, checklists, and rubrics for that type of writing. My colleagues, especially in middle school, tell me, "We're all in with CER (claims, evidence, and reasoning)." But often that statement is followed with, "But I'm not sure the kids really like writing." Rather than working through how to write a persuasive essay, this chapter offers strategies to incorporate what students learned and enjoyed while writing fiction into persuasive power tools. Award-winning editorials and essays employ more than just a claim, supporting evidence, and reasoning. It's tools from the narrative toolbox, like imagery and fig-urative language, that elevate an argument into something memorable and profound.

 Day 1

Warm-Up – Piece of Cake

Post images of one or more types of cake slices. The prompt: *Convince an adult that this is a healthy breakfast.*

Rather than the usual short sharing routine, this warm-up calls for some dramatic reading. Get students into pairs and trios to read aloud their pleas and arguments in favor of cake for breakfast.

Invite students to look at what they wrote and think about what they heard. Which persuasive techniques did they and their fellow writers use and use most frequently?

Experts Cited

- 87% of nutritionists surveyed said cake was an excellent option for breakfast.
- Dr. Anthony Fauci has been known to enjoy a slice of cake first thing in the morning.

Strong, Precise Vocabulary

- Vanilla pound cake, with its higher concentration of sugar, eggs, and butter, offers a calorie-rich breakfast for those needing a portable option.

Imagery

- Picture yourself celebrating breakfast every day with a delicious slice of cake.
- Cake turns every morning into a birthday party.

Figurative Language

- No longer will your sweet dreams crumble like cinnamon topping when you can start each morning with cake.

Repetition

- Cake for breakfast, yes, cake as the first meal of the day is as easy as, well, a piece of cake.

Reasons/Data

- Cake is nearly identical in nutritional content to other breakfast foods such as donuts, muffins, and cereal.

- Dietitians stress the importance of starting off the day with a hunger-satisfying meal.

Address Objections

- Some adults think cake is "too sweet" and "full of empty carbs," but a sugar boost is often what growing humans need to jump start their metabolism and their brains in the morning.

Storytelling

- When Alex was young, he struggled to wake up each day. He often skipped showers, forgot to pack his lunch, missed the bus, and left his homework at home. Alex's parents tried everything, including making him go to bed right after dinner. But nothing worked, not even coffee. One morning, alone in the kitchen, Alex found the cereal box empty. On the counter was the leftover chocolate cake from his grandpa's birthday. Not seeing any other breakfast options, Alex helped himself to a delicious slice and wow, he felt great. Not only was he full but he was happy and, best of all, awake! Though he was worried about getting in trouble for eating Grandpa's cake, Alex told his dad how great he felt. Reluctantly, his father agreed to let Alex have cake for breakfast on Monday morning. Sure enough, it worked! And now with cake in hand each day, Alex is clean, on time, and keeping up his grades.

Mini-Lesson – Exploring Options for Persuasion

Invite students to choose one of the following techniques and apply it to a different situation. [Some students will want to keep writing about cake for breakfast and that's fine.]

Brainstorm ideas as a class. Other examples might be convincing adults about:

- A later bedtime on weekends
- More screen time
- Fewer vegetables
- More time for P.E. at school
- Less time for P.E. at school
- The importance of taking field trips once a week
- E-sports are the same as physical sports

 # Day 2

Harness the Power of Analogy

Warm-Up – The Bed Jet Commercial

Search YouTube for one of the earlier Bed Jet commercials. "See How a Device Called BedJet Is Helping Couples Fight Less, Rest More, and Enjoy Bedtime Again." (YouTube, BEDJET, 2018, www.youtube. com/watch?v=zXjIY-j8Yyw.) This is about a couple who have different sleeping temperatures and the product that can solve this problem. This commercial is full of figurative language and humor and is also totally convincing. The husband, Carl, is portrayed as "a devil, not *the* devil" and is not in any way scary, but definitely pre-watch keeping specific students in mind. Another very funny commercial is for the Squatty Potty and might be more suitable for younger students; however, it is about pooping. "This Unicorn Changed the Way I Poop." YouTube, The Squatty Potty, 2015 https://www.youtube.com/watch?v=YbYWhdLO43Q.)

As students watch, have them track the analogies used "like sleeping in a cloud." Explain that a key purpose of analogy is to make something unfamiliar understandable. Working alone or in pairs have students write a new analogy that might help sell the BedJet.

Mini-Lesson – Using Analogy for Persuasion

Definition of analogy:

> "An analogy is a literary technique in which two unrelated [things] are compared for their shared qualities. Unlike a simile or a metaphor, an analogy is not a figure of speech, though the three are often quite similar. Instead, analogies are strong rhetorical devices used to make rational arguments and support ideas by showing connections and comparisons between dissimilar things." *Literaryterms.net*

Offer six options for writing practice today. Students should try at least two. For each practice, they should write between one to three sentences depending on where the analogy falls and if it needs framing with supporting ideas. Some students already use analogies, at least while speaking, if not in writing. For these students, push them to go beyond cliché and into specifics. For example, *dropped it like a hot potato* is a very common analogy. *Dropped it like a live tarantula* is less common but still incorporates the same hand gesture.

Persuade someone to: buy something, go somewhere, do something
Buy - workout equipment
Go - to Iceland
Do - recycle

Persuade someone NOT to: buy something, go somewhere, do something
Buy - expired holiday candy
Go - to the haunted house
Do - not have open fires while camping

Some students might need more practice with common examples of analogies. Advertising is usually a rich source of material, but some of the narrative nonfiction mentor texts will have excellent examples to revisit as well.

Call the class back together to share out and celebrate the good and probably funny writing that many produced. Then spend a few minutes thinking about where analogies might fit in a standard five-paragraph essay.

Day 3 – Perspectives on Places

When I first started thinking about persuasive writing and narrative tools, I thought about essays about places. Specifically, travel writing that might lure a person to visit an otherwise risky locale. Or writing that might dissuade a family from moving to a certain area.

Warm-Up – Safety First

Use a picture of a stop sign on one half of the screen and a picture of a green light on the other half. Prompt: *List adjectives to describe a safe place, then list adjectives to describe a dangerous place.* Instead of the usual sharing routine, ask students to compare lists in groups of four until each person has seven to ten adjectives on both lists.

Next post pictures of the following: a hospital, an amusement park, a zoo, and a construction site.

Ask students to look at their lists and think about how to describe a place that might be considered either safe or dangerous, depending on your point of view.

Practice together with one of the places by making a t-chart. On one half of the chart, list at least three reasons why a hospital would be considered a "safe place" for a field trip. On the other half, list at least three reasons why a hospital would be considered a dangerous place for a field trip. If students get stuck on reasons, they should check their adjectives list for ideas.

Writing Practice

Invite students to come up with three bigger reasons either a place used for the warm-up or a different place would be a great/terrible field trip. Then challenge them to find three specific details to expand their reasoning. Time permitting, challenged them to expand these into sentences and paragraphs.

Example:

Three reasons we shouldn't go to the hospital for a field trip: Germs, People under stress, No access to the cool stuff

- Germs – in the air, on surfaces, in fluids that might spill.
- People under stress – doctors and nurses rushing around, families waiting and worrying, possibly sad, patients hurrying to and from appointments.
- Access blocked to the cool stuff –can't watch surgery, can't see people getting treatment, not able to get a realistic view of what medical professionals do every day.

Practicing generating three macro reasons with three sub-reasons each will help students be ready for the type of persuasive writing most commonly found on state assessments. Using what students have already learned about how to build setting in fiction might move students closer to success. Plus, thinking about field trips is almost always fun.

Extension for Older/Advanced Students

Recently, I've been listening to a podcast called "You're Wrong About" by Michael Hobbs and Sarah Marshall. Some of the language and topics are for adults, so don't just turn students loose to listen. But the idea of something from history or a big concept like, "Why are clowns scary?" needing to be aired out and examined to prove what the general public thinks/thought (and/or was told) was wrong, has the earmarks of a much more interesting type of persuasive piece to write. Students and my own children love to tell me when I'm wrong or when someone else was wrong. Between their sense of justice and their love of deep research dives, some students might enjoy the chance to write an essay in which they persuade the reader they've been wrong about…

Ask Your Students

Ask students how familiar they are with the strategies and approaches for persuasive writing. Get curious about their favorite parts and what they liked the least. Find out how many minutes of total writing time was spent on persuasive writing the previous year.

Ask them where they see persuasive writing in the world. Most of them read/listen to/watch reviews of products they're interested in. Some of them have read opinion essays by journalists and guest contributors to various newspapers and online publications, usually for school, but maybe with certain family members.

Social media has many outlets for opinion pieces but they're generally all shorter than a traditional essay. Explore with students the differences and similarities between what they see on social media and formal written essay requirements for school.

Ask Yourself

Can you pre-assess for persuasive writing and move through the practice and products quickly?

What does proficiency in persuasive writing look like for the grade level you teach?

What does mastery of persuasive writing look like for the grade level you teach?

What was your data last year on high stakes writing assessments for persuasive writing? Does the work and time spent match the data outcomes? Why or why not? (Just kidding – don't write an essay response, just think about the data and the students from last year and consider how to enhance what worked and ditch what didn't work.)

For standards-aligned writing instruction, persuasion/argument should consume about 33% of the writing year. So, how flexible can you be with the topics students want to write persuasive essays about? *This is the best place to start to generate interest.*

Would the option to play with narrative techniques within the structure of argument coax some of those writers into stronger nonfiction efforts and outcomes? Can you align the persuasive writing assignments more closely with the types of persuasive writing students are most interested in, like reviews?

Be mindful of building, district, and state requirements. But also consider that too much of one kind of writing instruction is as unhealthy and restrictive as any unbalanced diet. This analogy doesn't apply to what students write in their free time, just to how minutes of writing instruction are spent over the course of the year.

In her book, *Study Driven*, Katie Wood Ray (Heinemann, 2006) talks about the origin of the word "essay" and its link to the idea of a journey. Does your persuasive writing instruction allow room for writing to be a thought journey or an idea journey?

Some younger students struggle with the logical flow of writing an argument because they aren't developmentally ready for that type of thinking. Remember learning how to structure proofs in Geometry? The logic/math kids were ready. The art/poetry kids were…less ready.

Could you differentiate persuasive writing instruction based on the need for structure?

Is your need for teaching writing with structure greater than your students' needs to learn through structure?

Next Steps for Gifted Writers

Being good at something doesn't mean they love it. But sometimes gifted writers are good at writing arguments *because* they love it. As you confer with writers this cycle, be sure to find out where gifted writers fall on the "writing for love vs. writing because I have to" continuum with regard to persuasive writing.

If gifted writers are happy being advanced for their grade level and have no interest in additional work/challenges in persuasive writing, let it go. The focus for the year is on growth as writers overall. Instead ask, after a successful pre-assessment of this unit, "What do you want to work on in writing at this point in the year? What is the best spend of your time in terms of your growth?"

If gifted writers do poorly on the pre-assessment of the persuasive writing unit, confer with them about what they need. Some might be frustrated that this is not a narrative cycle, some might only be able to write to certain topics, some might feel hampered and confused by required structures, like internal citation. Gifted writers who struggle with argument are still gifted writers and will need more targeted instruction for this unit than general education students might.

Gifted writers who love writing arguments will want more. More mentor texts, more opportunities to write, more complex topics, etc. Point these writers toward the archives of award-winning essays. Invite them to think about when breaking traditional structures works and when it doesn't. Complex topics can be found everywhere in current events, but also in the archives of national debate and forensics competitions.

In an NAGC session long ago, Michael Clay Thompson was presenting about the great essays and great speeches from history. He asked us something like, "Who is writing the non-fiction that calls people to lay down their lives?" You might invite the gifted argument writers to investigate this question through a historical lens and perhaps try to write something along those lines.

Next Steps

Next Steps for Struggling or Reluctant Writers

I once had a student who would only write about the Nebraska Huskers football team. When we got to persuasive writing, it was an easy decision to have him write arguments about who the best quarterback in team history was or why the Huskers did or did not deserve to go to a bowl game in a given year and so forth. This student wasn't reluctant so much as he only wanted to write about what he loved and he only loved one thing in 7th grade.

Reluctant writers might be motivated by choice during the study of persuasive writing more than any other time. Let them write about which dogs make the best pet or which cool sneakers are worth the money. One year a student wrote a fascinating piece about which coaches, specifically those new to the NBA, were likely to make a difference with their teams win-loss records this season. It was the deepest thinking I'd ever gotten from this student and I learned a bunch.

Struggling writers are the ones most likely to benefit from heavily structured supports, but they won't like the supports any more than other students. Using television ads as mentor texts might be a better fit and make an easier connection. Many ads list three reasons why their fast food restaurant or their pizza is better. Often the three reasons are taste, low cost/high value, nutrition. Choose an ad and then model scribing the three reasons and any elaboration provided, for example nutrition might include fresh vegetables, real cheese, and sauce made with vine-ripened tomatoes. Draw this out and practice converting what the ad said or showed into sentences. Modeled talk and modeled writing may work best here. Remember to be as flexible as possible about topic choices in service to students developing the skill of building an argument.

Write What You Want to Learn
Interest-Based Technical Writing

Informational writing, sometimes called technical writing, appeals to students who like to know things as well as students who like patterns and structure. It's difficult, depending on the constraints of a curriculum map or program, to separate out true informational writing from fact-regurgitation as the "proof of knowledge" product in a given unit.

This type of writing, like all others, should start with a choice. An open-minded approach to informational writing, especially separating the writing procedure from the topics students choose, will make a major difference in how students feel about the task. Holding a scientific concept, or a piece of history up to the light and examining its facets creates a different feeling in the writer than assigned lists in paragraph form detailing the major exports of Uruguay. A thoughtful approach to interest-based technical writing can create one of those rare moments when students remember that school is a place to learn. Bonus, learning how to learn what you want to know, versus what your teacher wants you to know, is a critical life skill.

The question that can stun a class to silence is "What do you want to learn?" Some students have an answer right away but depending on their age and how much they trust you they may not be inclined to share. A related question is "What are you interested in and want to know more about?"

At its core, the purpose of technical writing is to convey information. It is the "just the facts ma'am" of genres. But everyone who read a textbook knows that "just the facts" writing can fall anywhere on the scale from nap-inducing to exciting. At first, it might seem like the difference would be the set of facts in question. The goal of this unit is to convince students the difference between snore and shout is not the topic, but the writing.

Technical Writing Day 1 – Explain a Procedure

Warm-Up

For younger students, show a picture of the library at your school and ask them to write down the steps of how to check out a book.

For older students, show a screenshot from the online grade book or whatever grading tool is most common in your building (no names or identifying info) and ask them to write down the steps of how to find out what their grades are in the middle of a quarter or semester, basically between progress reports or report cards.

They can do this with a list, with bullets, with a flow chart – whatever makes the most sense to them. Some might include photos or diagrams or screenshots.

Mini-Lesson

A key purpose of technical writing is to explain a procedure.

Think together as a class about when they have followed the instructions for a procedure. Did the instructions generally work? Explain that a critical component of writing down a procedure is testing it to make sure you didn't forget any steps. Ask older students about "life hacks." Have they tried any? Which ones worked?

Next, ask for volunteers to test the procedure written for warm-up. Choose two volunteer testers. The catch? The testers don't get to test their own steps, they have to use the steps written by someone else. Choose two sets of directions at random and give one to each volunteer.

While the volunteers are testing (a paraprofessional might need to follow along to support younger students testing the library procedure), group the class into 2's and 3's to compare written procedures from the writing warm-up and formatting. Direct students to look for procedures that included additional helpful content, e.g., "the name of the librarian is____."

When the volunteers are ready to report out, ask them to do so in terms of what worked, what didn't work, what was needed, and what was unnecessary. What you will likely discover as a group is that explaining a procedure with the "just right" amount of information can be tricky.

Technical writing starts with the identification of a need. Ask the class to think about what other procedures at school might seem obvious to teachers and students who have been there a while, but might seem confusing to newer staff and students or visitors. For older students, you might expand this to other procedures in the community (public library, rec center, car wash, reserving picnic areas at local parks, reserving camp sites, etc.).

School websites are a great place to evaluate for technical writing. My personal frustration with school websites is that schools have four categories of people going in and out their doors: staff, students, parents, and visitors. Yet, most websites assume that the person viewing the main page is either a staff member or a parent. As a result, many (and I mean *many*) school websites do not include start and stop times on the home page. Sometimes that information is buried three or four clicks into the site and sometimes it's not there at all. That makes it super tough for a visitor like me to figure out when the parking lot will be slammed with cars, for example.

For this next exercise, use the website for your building or a school in a different town. Sometimes it's easier to see what's missing when the place is not familiar.

Ask students to pretend they are a family moving into the neighborhood who wish to visit the school. Ask them to assess what information is included and useful for new families and what might be missing. A second option is to have students pretend they are a guest speaker coming to speak to a specific class, such as a meteorologist talking with a specific science class taught by a specific teacher. Have them evaluate the information on the school's website about bell times, parking, checking into the building, showing ID, etc. Is it easy to find? Easy to understand?

The purpose of this exercise is to illuminate the challenges of technical writing and to demonstrate how technical writing for websites can vary immensely, even in a common category, like schools.

Working in 2's and 3's, assign students the task of writing a new webpage (or revising the current page) for either families new to the area or visitors to the school. Students may have some ideas about how these ideas could be tested, just as they tested the library procedure or the checking grades procedure. One of the biggest stumbling blocks of technical writing is that it does not always get tested and therefore can remain unclear.

A variation on this assignment is for students to evaluate the web content of a place they plan to go, like the museum or an amusement park, or a place they've been recently. As students move into more professionally done websites, they will need to be reminded to focus on the information they seek and how easy or difficult it is to find. The graphics and transitions will make the website seem better than the relatively plain school websites, but fancy design cannot compensate for bad writing or the absence of clear information.

For thinking homework, invite students to ask their parents about the technical writing they've done for work, or the technical writing (especially on websites) they've found particularly useful or particularly frustrating.

Day 2: Present a Problem/Provide a Solution

The present a problem/provide a solution type of technical writing requires baseline knowledge which usually necessitates at least a little research by students.

Warm-Up

Use a picture of a touchless water bottle filler, either attached to a water fountain or not.

Prompt: *Pretend you are employed by a company working on a solution for filling water bottles ten years ago. How would you describe the problem?* (Younger students may not remember a time when water bottle fillers weren't available at schools, but they've probably visited places without them.) After the sharing routine, ask students to break down and describe how the touchless water bottle filler solves several problems and to attempt to describe the technology as they do so.

Mini-Lesson

Present a problem/provide a solution is another common type of technical writing often found in the tech industry and other places as well. As students explore this aspect of technical writing, they might see how it could bleed into advertising. Problem/solution technical writing also leans toward science writing. In the tech industry, writers might need to simplify and explain a breakthrough, how it was discovered, and what it does that advances the "thing," whatever that thing might be. But that's different than capturing an entire procedure step-by-step.

I recently saw an excellent example of this on the website for a protein bar company. Two major problems with protein bars are that they often taste yucky and they often have a dry, cardboard texture. A protein bar that does taste good and/or has a pleasing texture usually has higher calories, carbs, or fat content than a diet-conscious consumer wants. On the webpage for this particular protein bar, the problem was laid out in the first paragraph. The next four short paragraphs went through each of the things this company had done to create a low calorie, low carb, low-fat protein bar that is shelf-stable and tastes great. The specific scientific methods were not spelled out. The sales pitch was not on this page either. Just five short paragraphs about the problem and the solution their company created.

Writing Practice

Students can work alone or in teams to research a product and then draft problem/solution technical writing about a product. Publications like *Popular Mechanics* and *Popular Science* have great lists of current innovations to jog thinking, but you might want to create a set of choices ahead of time. One item that caught my interest was "lab grown meat," which refers to products like the new lab-created chicken by Eat Just, Inc. Most of the mentor texts you need to support this version of technical writing will be available on product websites. As you're conferring and supporting students, you will need to remind some of them that technical writing does not have "voice" as it's defined by the Six Traits +1 rubric.

Day 3: Make a Concept or Issue Easier to Understand

Warm-Up

Show images or a few words that convey a complex topic related to either current events, new technology, or for elementary teachers, the science or social studies content.

Prompt: *choose one of the topics on the screen and write an explanation for a five-year-old.*

As students are sharing out, you're going to hear a range of attempts. Some students will over-simplify both the concept and the vocabulary. Some won't break down the ideas far enough. Be ready with your own example(s). You can find good, short "explain like I'm five" videos on YouTube, as well as great examples via a quick internet search. Current "how things work" books are also great mentor texts for this kind of technical writing.

Mini-Lesson

An overarching goal of technical writing is "to make the complex, simple." Years ago, *Explain Like I'm Five* became popular on Reddit and other forums because those posts met the goal of making something complex, like the Electoral College or how bone conduction microphones work, simple enough to understand for a person with no background knowledge.

In the history of technical writing, this is where the idea of a "white paper" originated. Legislative aides in congressional offices would write up the key components of a bill or a local problem and then list several possible outcomes, slanting the options toward the best one for the municipality or group with the problem. White papers can be found in many career fields now, including education, but it's rare that students have access to this type of technical writing prior to college.

Where technical writing diverges from the traditional "how to" writing or "all about" writing is in its specificity, the absence of "voice," and its goal. When I was teaching how-to-writing, my students wrote how to____ about things that really weren't worth the time to explain, like how to make a sandwich. Technical writing explains things people truly a) wouldn't understand on their own and b) need to know in order to be successful in X career or X situation.

As a class, brainstorm, a list of ideas and activities that if broken down and explained properly could allow more individuals to deepen understanding and gain expertise. You might have a second list of ideas that are often misunderstood and would benefit from clear technical writing.

Coaching soccer, running a restaurant, and excavating fossils are all activities for which technical writing can be found. Ideas like air quality, school ratings, and universal health care are tossed around in local news stories, but what do those phrases mean?

Writing Practice

Give students time to both research a concept/process and to begin drafting. Based on your knowledge of the students, push as many as possible into writing about something they know little about. Part of the purpose of the exercise is to experience technical writing from scratch. For example, the writers who produce content for a car company's website are not the engineers who designed the cars. The website writers have to gather information about the cars and then turn that into something non-car-designing experts and potential car purchasers will understand.

Depending on the time you have for this work, technical writing could lend itself to a longer project, particularly in conjunction with content from another discipline. Students can choose which of the three types of technical writing they like best and create a *slightly* longer piece. Technical writing is intended to be concise and should not be confused with research papers.

What about infographics? Yes, this is a perfect example (and students will likely point this out) of when a table or graph gives an easier-to-understand explanation than sentences can convey. Adding infographics will be a challenge for some students and a helpful scaffold for others.

Ask Your Students

What do they notice about writing out in the world? And if that's too general, ask, what types of writing do they see the most often? Websites and advertising should come up along with books. Newspapers are mostly online as are many magazines. A few will mention comic books and possibly web comics.

Ask if they might consider writing for a job. If nothing else, studying technical writing demonstrates how many jobs and career options are out there for writers who like information, procedure, and making complex things easier to understand. Technical writing provides procedures for teaching oneself many things.

At the end of this section, ask students what they're noticing about themselves during writing time. If they're not sure, point out how well they're doing with notebook routines and sharing routines. Also, highlight some of the good writing you've read while conferring. Hopefully, you will hear that writing feels easier or more fun or at the very least, *less bad*.

Ask Yourself

Which types of technical writing do I read/use in my adult life?

Have I been asked to produce technical writing?

How does technical writing compare to teaching/explaining? Similarities and differences?

Technical writing shows up in most state and national standards as it connects to the broader categories of informational writing and research. And technical writing is a skill set needed across multiple industries. Part of the inspiration for this chapter came from a literacy team colleague who out-of-blue said, "In my entire career, including getting my Ph.D., I haven't needed to write a five-paragraph essay." She wasn't meaning to put down the five-paragraph essay so much as was thinking out loud about the connection between writing at school and writing in the world as an adult.

Earlier in this book, I mentioned how the most visible result of professional writing in a school is in books. But websites are a close second. Without a bit of focus and study, however, do students consider the text found on websites as writing? Some students might think along the lines of "the internet wrote it" or "robots wrote it." And that would be incredibly cool. But humans write all the text on websites, at least for now, and that's a solid job option in many industries.

In school, we strive to show students all the ways they might use math in life. And we definitely point out all the places where reading will be critical and necessary. But do we do this with writing? Some teachers try. I know many who include lessons on writing emails and resumes and other practical applications for basic grammar, punctuation, and sentence structure. But other teachers put writing in you-have-to-do-this-because-it's-school box. For the students who aren't storytellers, but who love to learn and explain things, technical writing might be what opens their eyes to an entire new set of options for professional writers.

Next Steps for Gifted Writers

Gifted people like to know things. But not all gifted people who know something and/or are good at something can *explain* it. Some gifted students will embrace technical writing because they can choose concepts or activities with no social or emotional content. But these same students may struggle to break down what – to them – is already simple. Encouraging these students to choose a less familiar topic is an excellent work around for this problem, but they may resist. Gifted people like to know things and they hate the feeling of *not knowing*. Attempting technical writing on a topic that is relatively new or unknown will feel like a hard stretch. This resistance is best handled during one-on-one writing conferences, definitely not something to call out or force in front of the larger group.

A related option is for the student to draft two pieces of technical writing, one on a familiar concept or activity, one on a new concept or activity, and compare the experience of writing from an insider versus an outsider perspective. Some people find they can be clearer and more objective when writing at a distance. Some people find that experience makes them better explainers and better at explaining where missteps and pitfalls might occur.

Next Steps

Next Steps for Struggling or Reluctant Writers

Sometimes people who have challenges see high value in helping others not to struggle. I've met a lot of reading teachers who were struggling readers as children, for example. Technical writing might bring out the altruism in reluctant writers and it might appeal to their wish for shorter options in writing assignments. It's often the reluctant writers who ask, "why does it have to be a paragraph when I can say what I need in one sentence?" For this reason, including an infographic as a modification to the technical writing assignment might be a good strategy. The student would still research. But instead of a page of writing, that student might create an infographic and write one to two sentences pointing out the critical data in the chart.

The altruistic struggling writers will be interested in writing about something that everyone else seemed to know but them. They might want to write about a procedure they found frustrating and were left with the "why didn't you just say so" feelings.

Schools seem to have as many unwritten norms as written ones. Invite reluctant writers to create technical writing for school spaces that might need more clear explanations, such as the gym, the playground, the water fountain by the main office, and so on. Then the students' published writing can be laminated and posted to help others. Check with the school administrators before posting, of course.

The Opportunity to Write

10 | Writing Minutes Versus School Schedules

When I'm presenting at literacy or gifted education conferences about all things writing, a teacher inevitably asks, "*When* do you do this?" And/or "*How* do you plan for all of this?"

Instructional minutes are precious.

Figuring how to fit in genre study, along with other types of writing, and a full publication cycle can seem overwhelming at first. For me, the critical guidepost is the standards. From there, I consider any curriculum maps or literacy programs a building or a district has committed to implement. And then I literally start drawing out plans. I'm a visual planner who can't draw a straight line, so I'll often create a table on a document to map out my thinking for the year, the semester, the unit, and then get down to a week at a time. Figure 10.1 shows how you might plan for and include all the types of writing in this book into your writing year. Figure 10.2 breaks this down into the writing schedule for a single week.

Another approach would be to start with a guaranteed, in-class, "writing minutes per week" for every student. We have decades of reading research documenting how many minutes a day/week/year spent reading by grade level make a positive difference and the long-term impacts on student success these minutes of independent reading practice will have. The same is true for writing. Students need to build writing stamina by having plenty of time each week to engage in the ***physical*** act of writing.

Not talking about writing.
Not planning writing.
Not doing worksheets about commas or clauses.

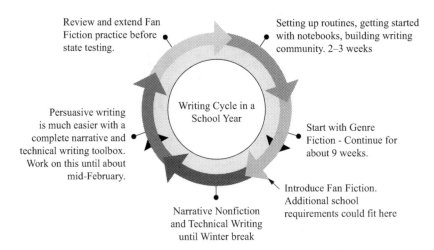

Review and extend Fan Fiction practice before state testing.

Setting up routines, getting started with notebooks, building writing community. 2–3 weeks

Writing Cycle in a School Year

Persuasive writing is much easier with a complete narrative and technical writing toolbox. Work on this until about mid-February.

Start with Genre Fiction - Continue for about 9 weeks.

Introduce Fan Fiction. Additional school requirements could fit here

Narrative Nonfiction and Technical Writing until Winter break

Figure 10.1 Writing cycle in a school year

My minimum is 70 minutes a week writing for intermediate grades, 40–50 minutes a week for primary grades. For middle school, 90 minutes a week will fit better in a block schedule. For those schools that don't block, 70–80 minutes a week should still fit, especially with Free Write Friday in the mix. Planning this way will change writing from an *event* in your classroom to a comfortable, integral *routine*. Bottom line, it can be done. Providing students with structured, supported opportunities to write on a daily and weekly basis will change their outcomes for the better.

In some of the earlier chapters, I suggested that you might shift certain types of writing into Social Studies and Science. This is much easier to do in an elementary, non-departmentalized setting. However, Social Studies and Science teachers have writing standards too. If you and your middle school team have a common plan time, you might find a way to incorporate writing across a student's day/week. A huge benefit of doing this across a team/department is the opportunity to develop a common language about writing and common expectations. Students tend to compartmentalize their learning into segments without cross-curricular support.

| Introduce Genre Mini Lesson 1 | Mini Lesson 2 Writing Practice | Mini Lesson 3 Writing Practice | Free Write Friday Writing Conferences |

Figure 10.2 Writing instruction over a week

Haven't we all heard some variation of, "my Science teacher doesn't make me use details?"

Writing happens in all academic disciplines. But the type of writing and the expectations for the writing does vary. It is a gift to learners to not only provide them with a complete writing toolbox but to be upfront and clear about which tools are necessary under which circumstances.

One other option is to sneak in writing minutes during reading work.

I created a conference session called "Teach Writing Like an Author," which is connected to a different session I developed with my dear friend, Dr. Bob Seney, called "Read Like a Writer, Write Like a Reader." The challenge is that most teachers learn to read like readers and to teach a form of reading where writing is admired at a distance, almost the way we admire fireworks. "Ooh! So pretty!" "Amazing!" "Wow!"

The necessary shift in a writing classroom is to admire the writing *and then ask,* "What did the writer do? How did the writer do that?" You might have been in a museum and seen art students sitting and sketching in front of famous works of art, approximating the craft, attempting the lines, the shading, the perspective, and so on. Or perhaps you watch cooking shows? What do cooks do? Taste, stir, check, adjust – all the way to the end of the recipe. Sometimes the first (few) attempts at making your aunt's holiday gravy don't work. However, each attempt teaches you/the cook something. Growing writers need to do this as well.

This is when your practice with mentor texts gets really granular. Writing like a reader is the act of keeping the audience and the purpose of the piece in mind as you write, or more likely, as you revise. Asking things like, "will the reader be scared, happy, or devasted at X part in the story?" If the feedback is yes, great! If not, *why not?* Writing isn't a magical skill given to a lucky few. It's practice and approximation and discovery – more like cooking or painting than fireworks.

Read Like a Writer; Write Like a Reader Lesson Ideas and Routines

Throughout this book, you'll find examples of mentor texts I love for observing and practicing particular types of writing or writing techniques.

The lesson ideas below are meant to be portable across levels of text, genres, and types of text.

Notice It, Name It, Try It

My favorite! I use this all the time!

As you're working through a text as a small group, like during book clubs or guided reading, or as a whole group, like during a read aloud, be prepared to stop and "notice" something cool the writer did which impacted how you felt. This means you have your writer's notebook out and ready during reading.

The first few years I did this, I was noticing the minutiae of writer's craft, choices in verbs, unusual adjectives, dialog, and character moments. Later, I was noticing structure, plot choices, tropes, character shifts, and story shapes.

In my writer's notebook, I would copy down the section I liked and label it.

"Aunt Agatha's face was as shiny as the seat of a bus driver's trousers." P.G. Wodehouse, *Carry On Jeeves* (Herbert Jenkins, 1925).

Invite everyone to write that down.

Next, name (and write down) what the writer did. *P.G. Wodehouse used a surprising and funny comparison to describe the aunt.* The advanced level of naming includes the why: *this surprising, funny, and unflattering comparison shows that the main character, Bertie does not like his aunt without coming out and directly stating, Bertie does not like his Aunt Agatha.*

Finally, think of another funny and surprising comparison, that is, unflattering for an aunt who has a shiny face "Aunt Agatha's face was a shiny as a puddle of newly leaked oil in the driveway."

Some people keep a three-column chart, like in Table 10.1, in their writer's notebooks:

Table 10.1 Notice It, Name It, Try It

Notice It	Name It	Try It

Some people do this by date or by the title of the current text under study.

Depending on the amount of time in a given reading section of the day, you might only have students notice things and copy them down during reading time. And then they can come back to the naming and trying part during writing time.

Pretty please, don't force this or assign it like, "You must notice at least three writer's craft things during reading time today." Instead try to model this with curiosity and wonder, like when you're walking around the neighborhood and suddenly notice the tree on the corner is blooming or a new mural is going up in the alley.

One of my favorite teachers is Michael Clay Thompson. He has produced some phenomenal books about literacy instruction for high potential, advanced, and gifted students. One of the things he says as he's highlighting a moment in a canon text, like *The Scarlet Letter* by Nathaniel Hawthorne (Ticknor, Reed, and Fields, 1850), is that none of the great writers did anything by accident. The Notice It, Name It, Try It routine is part of unlocking the mystery of writing and calling attention to the choices and craft behind the beautiful, brilliant, funny, and amazing things we read.

Mini-Lesson – Words, Words, Words

Writers savor words the way a cook savors fresh basil from the garden. Another technique in reading like a writer is to collect and savor certain choice words that enhance understanding and make a sentence or phrase stand out from the rest of the paragraph.

The Words, Words, Words routine (thanks, Shakespeare) is related to Notice It, Name It, Try It, but focuses specifically on word knowledge as the foundation of good writing.

While Word Choice is one of the original Six Traits of Writing and many books have been written about Content Vocabulary, the *reading like a writer* move helps student writers understand *why* teachers care about these things. Sometimes I worry that when I thought students were learning, they were actually just mimicking and reproducing writing, kind of like how I was in Algebra class. Instead of transforming how a writer constructs a sentence, word choice is at risk to become another formula for the student to replicate: this number of strong verbs, this number of high-value adjectives, reduce the number of adverbs, etc.

For younger writers, a good place to begin word collection and savoring is in nonfiction texts. Some of these lovely words will absolutely be part of content vocabularies, like migration or photosynthesis. But as you read articles and textbook sections together, you can point out other words that in their specificity, make the meaning more clear.

This routine has lots of options. One is to collect the best, most juicy words you notice in a chart or on the word wall. The act of collecting and celebrating interesting and powerful words will have an impact on what students notice when they read.

The next option is to copy the word and also the sentence in which it appears. Take the awesome word out and observe how the sentence changes, how meaning is lost.

The final option is to look for patterns of word choices over the course of a paragraph, a section, or a chapter. Certain canon writers and modern writers too will choose words not only for their meaning but for their sounds. This is a cool and sneaky trick, and to find it requires reading out loud and listening for sh, sh, sh or kuh, tuh. Soft sounds versus sharp sounds can underscore the theme, mood, or tone of a piece of writing (not just for poetry!).

Inviting students to zoom in on words while reading moves them another step in the quest to become a master builder, like we were talking about earlier in the context of *The LEGO Movie* (Lord, Phil, et al. Warner Bros., 2014).

Just like the right amount of basil is perfect but too much basil overpowers the dish, so do too many amazing words in a single sentence or paragraph. Older students reading canon texts might accidentally associate beautiful, powerful words with the multi-syllabic SAT words they find. A super cool vocabulary word might feel fancy, like a super obscure ingredient in a complicated recipe. But sometimes those words (or those ingredients) get in the way of understanding and appreciation.

Cooking and building are both good analogies to use when playing with words. The goal of the Words, Words, Words routine is to help students find balance and harmony as they practice integrating rich and powerful vocabulary into their writing.

Gut Check!

The Gut Check routine is a twist on the more common reasons for annotation. Great writing, no matter the topic or genre, elicits an emotional response in the reader. This skill is definitely attainable by student writers as any teacher who has cried over students' essays or fiction knows.

Gut Check will take some modeling and normalizing of talking about emotions while talking about reading. "This essay made me so angry. Right here where it's talking about how developers ignored precautions about landfills...." Or "At the end of this chapter when the character is walking out of hockey practice alone, I felt lonely too."

When modeling the routine, the teacher notes the section where the emotion hit her in the guts and what the emotion was. Then she pokes at the text looking for where/how the writer evoked that emotion. Was it the words? Was it the dialog? The setting? The examples?

One sticking point with Gut Check is that emotional responses to text are personal. Not everyone will feel the same feelings and not everyone will be comfortable discussing feelings. This might be a routine to practice as a whole group and then follow-up with individuals or small groups later.

At some point in revision, a question to ask is about the writer's goal for the piece. Depending on the genre, the writer might have an emotional response goal such as, "I want to make people laugh."

Practicing the Gut Check routine during reading is also a twist on the Writer's Purpose conversation. After reading a piece, ask students to consider if part of the writer's purpose was to make the reader experience a specific emotion.

Ask Your Students

Ask your students to estimate how many minutes a week they spend in the physical act of writing. By now it's probably over 120 minutes, at least during your class. Next ask students to estimate how many minutes of writing they do in the other content areas: Math, Science, Social Studies, World Language, Art, Music, and Drama. This will vary by year and by teacher, but as students share out, patterns will emerge.

Next, ask students to think about a new skill they learned and then mastered through practice. Flip turns in swimming? Dribbling a basketball with the non-dominant hand? Playing the violin? You might also ask about video games. Students don't always think about games as a context within which they're practicing skills, but winning *Hyrule Warriors: Age of Calamity* (Developed by Omega Force, distributed by Nintendo, 2020) takes practice. Practicing skills inside a game – all the combinations of buttons, how to interact with NPC's – takes time and patience, just like writing.

For most of your students writing will never be as fun as games, BUT the writing practice can be silly and exciting and challenging in a good way. And just like any other skill, the more time they practice, with support and coaching, the better and more comfortable they will be with all the components of writing. The hope is, of course, that students grow to be life-long writers. All these instructional minutes spent on writing will make a positive difference, I promise.

Ask Yourself

What are the school/district goals for the year? What are the department goals or measured outcomes, specifically, what is the data you are responsible for? Schools and departments tend to set goals about writing based on the prior year's data. Sometimes the data is a downward trend in writing scores on ELA exams. But often if writing is trending down in ELA, students are losing points for poorly written responses on other content area exams as well.

For students to grow as writers, they must have guaranteed and reliable time to write weekly, if not daily. For students to grow as writers, they must have instruction in multiple types of writing.

District, school, and department goals can motivate individual teachers to work together to problem-solve around finding time for meaningful writing minutes and writing instruction in the schedule.

That's the big picture.

But for you, what do you wish for your writers? Whether this is your first year of teaching or your fifteenth, what kind of engagement and growth are you hoping to see in student writers? The reason I ask is that many veteran teachers I know, when they don't agree with the big picture goals, close their classroom doors and carry on as they always have with the occasional lip service to whatever the folks in the "head shed" are requiring.

So, while goals can unite teachers and support problem-solving about best uses of instructional time, the truth is, it comes down to the individual teacher and their drive to grow writers, or not.

Confession, my first four years of teaching I believed only in "the essay." I used writing minutes for informational and persuasive nonfiction. Then my principal told the Language Arts department that we had to attend a full week training by the Colorado Writing Project. Even though I began with reluctance, learning from our facilitator and teachers with much more experience was transformative. I left believing that my students needed more time to write, more choices, and more purposeful instruction in writing.

But it was really hard finding resources to support my fledgling ideas. Writer's workshop is a fantastic structure, but what was I supposed to do inside that structure, so I wasn't wasting the minutes taken away from reading canon novels and writing literary analysis?

Katie Wood Ray's book on Writer's Workshop (NCTE, 2001) led me to her book *Study Driven* (Heinemann, 2006). She offers a simple rule that has guided my writing instruction and my own writing ever since.

Study the Thing You Want to Make.

It's really that simple. Want to write Fantasy novels? Read a lot of fantasy. Break it down into components, test and try the components you like best. Write a lot of fantasy.

Study Driven, more than any other book about writing, provided granular ideas about what to actually do during writing time, and more importantly gave me permission to do what I naturally do. My default is always to use the standards as a frame and ask my students what they want to learn and how they would know they got better at reading and writing by the end of the year.

All these years later, I'm writing this book for the teacher I was then, the novice who was cobbling together ideas and teaching by the seat of her pants.

Funny, that expression "by the seat of your pants" applies to writers too. Some writers identify as planners, some as "pantsers," and some as "plantsers" which are people who plan at least a little but leave room for plot and character spontaneity. No matter which one of those you are as a teacher or teacher/writer, I hope you're seeing lots of new writing from your students this year.

Next Steps

Next Steps for Reluctant or Struggling Writers

It takes a while for students who think they hate writing to open up to the idea that writing doesn't always have to be terrible. A small victory I had one year was when a particularly struggling student told me that he now thought, "writing sucked less." For your reluctant writers continue to celebrate all the words produced. Be as open as possible to every tiny request and idea. Can I write about zombies? Yes. Can I write about gummy bears? Yes. Reluctant writers having ideas about writing is a victory because this means the students are opening up to trying writing.

Last year, I heard the author Matt de la Peña speak at a literacy conference. He describes himself as bilingual, biracial, and bicultural. In school, his main outlet was sports until one teacher pulled him aside and told him how good of a writer he was. One teacher saw his potential in high school and when basketball didn't turn into a career, he remembered what that teacher said and decided to give creative writing a try.

My belief is that I might have the next Dav Pilkey or the next Sabaa Tahir in my class. Too many now-professional writers post about how they became writers in spite of their teachers. Be like Matt de la Peña's high school English teacher and encourage *potential* to expand.

Next Steps for Gifted Writers

Revisit the chart of writerly activities and ask gifted writers to think about how their time is divided amongst those things. Are they allocating most of their writing minutes to drafting? If not, they are probably researching or revising. Depending on the word count they're producing, some constraints, especially around revision, might be needed.

The early years for gifted writers should be dedicated to getting down as many words, in as many genres, as possible. However, coaxing them to try all the things and to stop revising at the word and sentence level can be difficult. Some might immediately commit to a single genre and not budge. If this happens, let it go. The default teaching stance is *writing is good. Keep writing*. But if you can get gifted writers to continue trying new things and to push themselves out to their thinking and feeling edge, the results may be astonishing. Over the years, I've had some truly marvelous surprises when students produced high quality, beautiful, powerful writing.

Revision, Sharing, and Publishing

What's changed in your writing community? What does it look like when students sit down to write? Hopefully, small celebrations have become routine and writers are able to engage with trusted partners to talk about ideas and ask revision questions. As all professional writers will at some point have to talk to others about their writing and read some of it out loud, it's important to offer this experience to your writers.

Those moments when I look across a group of developing writers clearly happy and busy and *trying* are worth every other moment of sweating over routines and finding just the right picture, video clip, or excerpt for a lesson. Small classroom joys are why I love this job so much. However, unless an administrator happens to be a co-witness or you have the option to submit video in place of mandated assessments, additional evaluation of writing will be necessary.

Some teachers will use this book to support a mandated writing curriculum or school-selected writing framework. But others will use this book because no writing curriculum has been provided. Will all this fun stuff get students ready for testing?

Yes.

If we were in person, I would look you in the eye and say this with conviction. Writing every day and becoming comfortable with a wide range of reasons to write, types of writing, and means of getting started makes a huge difference when it comes to a high-stakes performance evaluation. However, a little practice and providing clarification between writing for tests and writing for class is important.

In the long run, all this fun stuff frontloads writing behaviors and writing expectations, as well as the schema and vocabulary for lifelong writing. Some of your students might become professional writers – novelists, journalists, technical writers, podcasters, or writing jobs we don't know about yet.

Revision

A few years ago, a teacher friend expressed frustration with the limited amount of revisions her creative writing students were doing. "They hate revision," she said.

> "I used to hate revision, but now I love it," I replied. "Revision is solving problems in the writing."
>
> "Well you come teach them then," she said. "Maybe since you're a stranger and a writer, they'll listen to you."

After opening my mouth, I knew I had to deliver. But where to start? This was a school that used essential questions for each lesson, so we decided to open with the question, "How and when do writers know to revise?" We invited students to discuss at their tables and then share out. We got some answers like, "when the writing is bad" and "when the story doesn't make sense." Another student offered, "When the story isn't how they want it yet." This gave me hope that these 8th graders absolutely did know the difference between line editing and true revision.

My colleague and I, taking inspiration from the NaNoWriMo noveling workbook for middle school writers (*NaNoWriMo's Young Writers Program*, ywp.nanowrimo.org/pages/writer-resources), came up with a short inventory for the students to use with the piece they intended to publish next.

1. What type of writing is this piece? For example, humor.
2. What was your overall goal? For example, to make people laugh, to make fun of Green Bay Packers' fans, to get better at satire.
3. Find at least one place in the piece of writing where you think you really hit your goal(s) and highlight it.
4. Find at least one place in the piece of writing where you're not sure you hit your goal(s) and highlight it.

5. Compare a section that's working well for the piece with a section that's not working. What do you notice?

6. Working on your own or with a partner, play around with the section that's not working and see if you can get it closer to a fit with the goal(s) of the piece.

In general, students responded well and revised more deeply. "Better than before," my friend reported.

A few years later, working with my own class, I found I needed additional examples to help my 6th graders increase their understanding of *how* to revise, but also, *why* revision made the writing stronger. Based on what I'd been seeing, I created two exemplars of revision. One was about revising for those gut-check moments, so the reader felt the emotion the writer intended them to feel. The other was about revising for clarity, by choosing different, more specific details.

I wrote a passage that was supposed to be sad-ish, in which the main character feels like she doesn't have any friends. (The issue with my no-example was that it was mostly telling the reader how the girl was sad.) Then I rewrote it. I gave both examples to my students. They noticed the revised version was longer. (But only by a few sentences, I swear!) I walked them through the choices I made, hoping to nudge the reader's emotions. They agreed that they could connect more with the feelings inside the main character with the revised example.

The other passage was one of those, "it was the best day ever!" types. But it didn't have any details specific to the main character, just very generic stuff. I rewrote it and yes, it was longer, but details are always about point of view. Like if you eat pizza every day, it's not a big deal. But what if you haven't had a slice of hot, melty goodness in over a year? The day you get a slice at a farmer's market with homemade, ultra-fresh sauce and three kinds of cheese might become a key part of a "best day." The 6th graders had fun choosing details to be a part of a "best day ever" for their main character.

Aligning revision to goals, rubric, and craft usually help with the "do we have to?" and the "it's already perfect" responses. But the motivation to revise will come from both within the writers and also through the behaviors and support of the writing community. As the teacher, this is a critical moment to keep the focus on growth instead of on grades.

The Expanded Sharing Routine

Every three weeks is about the right interval to offer public, whole class sharing. This should also coincide with a three-week publication cycle. About a third of the class shares at a time. What I typically say when asked about sharing is: "For those of you who love to share, the bad news is, you only share about once a quarter. For those of you who hate sharing, the good news is, you only have to share about once a quarter."

Professional writers have to share their writing out loud. And most writers are introverts. It's not easy. And yet, it's important to get a little practice in a safe, structured environment.

To determine who shares and in what order, I first ask who really wants to share at the first opportunity and usually get enough volunteers to fill the spots. Try to have no more than ten students share on a given day. Otherwise, it just gets too long and the class loses focus and ability to provide useful feedback. For the other two sharing days in the quarter, I assign each remaining student a number and draw them randomly until I have a batting order.

- Before sharing day, make sure you have plenty of sticky notes.

- Confer with each of the sharing writers so they're ready with a working title for the piece they're sharing, have decided which 300–600 words they intend to share, and know what question they will ask for feedback from the class.

- Explain to the class that they will be giving feedback via sticky notes. Their feedback will be limited to answering the writer's question and offering either an "I wonder" or "I noticed" statement. You might want to practice with a few examples to help clarify how to be constructive. Also, students must put their initials at the bottom of the sticky note in case the writer can't read their writing. (And also for accountability, in case someone decides to be rude.)

- Emphasize that as the audience they are responding to the *writing*, not the *writer*. Not everyone gets along in a given class or classroom, so reminding everyone the purpose of feedback is *to help the writer grow*, is important.

On sharing day, which is usually a Thursday, each writer stands or sits in front of the class and says the following when it's their turn:

> My name is_____. (And spell it, if needed)
> The title of my piece is _____. (Also spelled out, if needed)
> The question I want feedback on is_____.

As the sharing student is saying these three things, the rest of the class is copying down the person's name, the title of the piece, and the question on a sticky note. This can alleviate the sense of being stared at since most of the audience members are looking down and writing.

- After the student shares, everyone claps. Always. This is important.

- Resist the urge to give oral feedback. Praise in front of the group is often almost as hard to bear as criticism.

- Thank the writer and dismiss them back to their seat while everyone finishes up their written feedback.

- Choose a student (especially one who needs movement breaks) to pick up all the sticky notes and take them to the writer who has just shared. The picking up sticky notes routine gives everyone a minute to catch their breath and get ready for the next writer. I choose a different student to pick up the sticky notes each time, to keep the busy kids busy.

- The writer who just shared should keep the sticky notes in their writer's notebook. (A sandwich bag stapled to the inside back cover is a good place to keep these.)

Sharing day is a powerful bonding day for a classroom writing community. Watching student writers being so brave and genuine as well as watching their classmates respond with kindness and support is awe-inspiring. Be sure to say a few words to this effect when either writing time or class time is over. If you are a treat-based rewards classroom, the first sharing day is a great opportunity for an extra Starburst or lollipop. Reinforce with sugar how wonderful you thought everyone was. They'll be sure to do just as well or better on the next sharing day in three weeks.

Grading

The Three-Week Publication Cycle

Several times now, I've mentioned that professional writing is about word counts and deadlines. Getting the words down and turning them in is a very important pair of habits. Set an expectation that students will publish one piece of writing no shorter than 300 words/about a page and no longer than 1500/about 5 pages every three weeks. For younger students consider adjusting the range to a minimum of 100 words and a maximum of 900.

What gets turned in can be anything we've been working on lately or a section of an ongoing, longer work in progress. Students should be choosing what they publish whenever possible. I've had students who turned in chapters of the same novel throughout the year. It's pretty amazing to watch a 6th grader press through the challenges of writing a book and get all the way to the end, in one case, a full 65,000 words.

The three-week publishing cycle quickly builds a portfolio, especially if you have the students all year. Between the 12 polished pieces of writing and the writers' notebooks, significant growth should be visible and measurable.

Rubrics

Not all writing rubrics are created equal. Some, including those produced for packaged writing curricula, are checklists in sentence form. I called it out earlier, but it's worth mentioning again that the Analytic Writing Continuum, created by the National Writing Project (Smith and Swain, Teachers College Press, 2017) is a great rubric if you don't have one that's working. It is flexible enough to be used for the types of writing required by state standards (narrative, informational, persuasive) but also shows the writer how to get better. The 6 Trait + 1 Rubric from the Northwest Regional Educational Laboratory also works nearly universally and has versions in primary-student friendly language.

If your school has a writing curriculum and a set of rubrics to go with it, use them. Just make sure they are the kind of rubrics that show a writer how to get better. Be cautious with any rubric that sounds like a formula: *this many of this type of word and this combination of these types of sentences.*

Definitely ask for or look for the writing rubric used for your state and other mandated assessments. It's important to give students some experience with how they will be graded on high stakes tests. That being said, state assessment rubrics tend to be quite general and don't show writers how to improve. Use them sparingly and in very specific I-need-you-to-know-this-for-the-test circumstances.

Self-Assessment Routine

Clarify which rubric will be used to assess the piece of writing that's due and which sections of the rubric will be the focus. [Do not use all sections of the rubric all the time. That's just too much.] When students turn in a piece of writing, they should highlight how they've scored themselves on the section or sections of the rubric being used this publication cycle. Using the same color, they should highlight an example or two in the piece that shows this work.

For example, in the section for Sentence Fluency on Analytic Writing Continuum, the descriptor for a 4 says, "The writing has some variation in sentence structure; fragments, if present, often work for stylistic purposes." A student who has highlighted that area of the rubric would also highlight a few places in the piece of writing that show sentence variation and the purposeful use of sentence fragments. Students may choose to self-assess in other areas of the rubric as well, but that won't impact their grade and you don't have to respond with additional feedback.

Peer-Assessment Routine

Just like peer conferences, creating the community for reliable and valid peer assessment takes time and trust. The use of the rubric is key here as well. After the writer has self-assessed, peer assessors should highlight descriptors on the rubric and corresponding sections of the peer's piece of writing as part of their feedback, e.g. "Roscio, this part here about squirrel hibernation, uses a good amount of scientific language, but also a simile. I'm going to highlight this section in Diction on the rubric which says 'contains words and expressions that are usually vivid and precise.'"

Practice this as a whole class with a piece of mentor text or a piece of your own writing that genuinely needs revision. When I'm demo-teaching, I always have works-in-progress that I genuinely need to confer about and for which I am seeking reader feedback.

*SEL Note: Not all students have skills in giving and receiving feedback. But all students can grow in these skills with practice. Receiving feedback is nearly as hard as sharing writing in public. Giving feedback in a constructive manner is an essential life skill. If certain students continue to struggle with these routines, consider bringing in a counselor to help with how you practice giving feedback together as a writing community.

Grading

Feedback and grades are both important because grades alone are less likely to help a writer grow. Separate the grade for grammar/spelling/punctuation from the rest of the writing grade. Conventions of language are very important for a final product but have only a limited connection to the quality of thought and expression in a piece of writing. The overall goal for students with challenges in the conventions of language is to grow in their ability to catch and correct their own errors. The grade in the grade book for each piece of published writing will be an aggregate of the student's self-assessment, the peer-assessment, and the teacher's assessment on the same rubric.

Other Y/N or Check, Check+, Check- Grades Might Include:

- A completion grade – was the work turned in?
- A grade for giving useful peer feedback.
- A grade for providing written feedback to all the writers on sharing day.
- Random notebook checks to verify students are at minimum, jotting down, and responding to warm-ups and mini-lessons.

Student Goal Setting and Reflection

At the end of week 2, you asked students to write down what their goals were in terms of how they hoped to grow as writers this year. After they've polished and turned in their first three pieces of writing, invite students to revisit their goals. Now that they've grown comfortable with whatever rubric is most frequently used, invite them to add language from the rubric to their goals.

Too many developing writers lack a sense of ownership over their writing progress. Providing an opportunity to focus on growth, "I'm getting so much better at using structure in my informational writing," versus achievement, "I got an A- on my last piece of writing," shifts the locus of control back to the writer.

 # End of the Term/Year Reflection

One purpose of writing that can be overdone is writing to reflect. While spontaneous reflection happens for many of us during rote activities like driving the same commute or showering, forced reflection doesn't always produce deep thought. Given all your students have attempted and accomplished over the past few months, use this time to celebrate and reflect on the huge range of learning opportunities you've created. Invite students to celebrate and reflect with you.

The best metacognitive activity for this is curating student writing portfolios along with your own. If you've been able to try something from every chapter of this book, students will have at least one short piece of fiction for each of the genres they tried. They should also have three pieces of nonfiction: narrative nonfiction, technical writing, and persuasive writing.

Reflection is quite different from revision. Students aren't looking at their earlier work to fix it. Instead, they're thinking about how they started and how much progress they've made. This conversation often begins with the concrete (word counts) and moves to the conceptual (the way you write about the setting can make a story a lot scarier). One of the best things a 7th-grade boy said as part of his reflection on his growth was, "Now I can just sit down and write."

Do not neglect the opportunity to revisit goals and writing from the earliest part of the term/year and celebrate growth and change. For fun, add up all the words written as individuals and then as a class. It will be a HUGE number of words. Put the number on a poster or somewhere public so that everyone can share in the accomplishment, or brag about it, or both.

Next Steps for Gifted Writers

Many gifted writers (and sometimes their parents) want to set contest wins and publication as a part of their goals. Word count goals, project completion goals, and craft goals generally make more sense for students not yet in high school. The publishing industry specifies that fiction for a middle-school audience or older must have a minimum word count of 55,000 words. Writing an entire novel is the only way to learn to write an entire novel, and for the rare gifted writer, this is the right goal. A related word count goal is around daily word count and daily writing habits. During NaNoWriMo, the daily word count goal is just over 1600 words/day. This is too high for many students; 300–600 words/day is more attainable, especially given the time constraints of other schoolwork and activities outside of school.

Another pitfall for gifted developing writers is the lure of writing the next great opening chapter. One phrase I learned from other writers was "beware of shiny new ideas." Beginnings are generally much more fun to write than middles and ends of stories. Sticking with a story idea until the end, while filing away all the other ideas, is a very important skill to practice. Yes, of course, some story ideas won't be able to sustain an entire novel. The only way to know this, to tune the writing instinct about which ideas will work and which won't, is to practice taking an idea through to completion.

Craft goals for developing writers are the most appropriate in many cases. Most need work on the structure of scenes versus chapters. Many need to work on dialog and dialog tags. Writing action, building setting, creating subplots, etc., are all options.

Related to goals are reflection and post-secondary and career planning. Most metropolitan areas have writing groups who offer conferences at least once a year. If the student is leaning more toward journalism or technical writing, connecting with a high school or local college journalism teacher would be a great opportunity to learn. Not all communities have local newspapers, but many do, and some offer internships and job shadowing options.

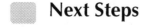 # Next Steps

Next Steps for Struggling or Reluctant Writers

Nearly every struggling or reluctant writer I've worked with has produced writing over the course of the year. Sometimes they find one thing and only write about that. Sometimes they write many tiny bits of writing without any commitment to a topic or genre.

Two keys for this group are:

- First that they continue to write and feel supported as writers.
- Second that they develop an internal locus of control about their own writing process.

Another important strategy for reluctant writers, which was mentioned earlier but bears repeating, is to restrict writing assignments to writing time only. For any other assessment or assignment that would have a short or long written answer as proof of reading comprehension or understanding the water cycle, provide an alternative. Many reluctant writers will complete these types of assessments verbally or using materials, like the icons for the water cycle, to show you they understand and can meet basic standards for the topic. A teacher stance like, "That's fine, I only need you to write during writing time," really helps. In middle school, this might take some conferring and planning as a team, but it can be done. While other content areas have writing embedded in their standards, the expectations are not as broad or extensive as the expectations in ELA. A reasonable goal for a reluctant writer might be that they complete 50% of the writing assessments in science by writing and 50% by an alternative means. Occasionally, reluctant writers prefer to write in Math, Science, or Social Studies and not during ELA/Literacy class. In this case, it's the ELA teacher who needs to be flexible and offer as many technical writing and non-fiction options as possible to provide support for the student to meet writing standards within their areas of interest.

12 | Identifying Gifted Writers

We don't have many roadmaps for identifying writers as gifted. Gifted identification in math and reading are well-traveled and well-documented, as are areas of creative production and the arts. But writing is both academic and creative; being gifted in writing requires **producing** writing, as part of the evidence of giftedness. Occasionally, we do have students who produce thousands of words of writing. This is often a good indication of raw talent and motivation, but not always an indication of giftedness. My argument is that when a writer has been without the means, motivation, and opportunity to write, we cannot say whether that person is gifted or struggling or just right for their grade level.

I once had the privilege of working with a teacher whose brilliant instruction and commitment to writers' workshop produced the highest test scores on state writing assessments in the district year after year. This wasn't because the gifted students were clustered in her class. It was because her teaching practices provided the means for students to develop gifted behaviors.

All the ideas contained in the previous chapters are to help surface and nurture writing talent in your classroom. Potentially gifted writers will adapt quickly to these new rhythms and routines as their writing stamina increases. You will soon have a large body of writing to compare with grade level and advanced rubrics. This body of writing might also go to your district/state level gifted experts depending on what local gifted identification procedures require. If you're not sure where to start looking for gifted writers, a good bet is to begin with students who love reading, who love language, and/or who are passionate, skilled verbal communicators. My best hope is that if you try the ideas and lessons in this book, the majority of your students will have the will and skill to write whatever they want, whenever they want. See Table 12.1 for the possible outcomes of the gifted identification process for writers.

What to include in a body of evidence for gifted identification in writing:

- Three or more polished pieces of writing –with rubrics showing scores significantly above grade level; writing from multiple years or parts of the year, if possible.
- State test scores from multiple years if possible, specifically writing scores.
- Student reflection on their body of work and goals as a writer.
- Home and Schools observations about the student's writing behaviors and choices.

How to evaluate a body of evidence for gifted identification in writing:

- Invite building or district writing and gifted experts to read through the writing samples and data with you.
- Look for patterns of consistent and persistent choices that the student will/has chosen writing to think, to express themselves, to create, during free time at school and home, etc.
- Ask, "What does this student need to grow as a writer?"
- State writing test scores below the 95th percentile do not automatically end the gifted identification in the writing process. Some gifted writers only write well for authentic, self-selected tasks.

Portfolio pitfalls:

- The writing has been heavily edited by an adult.
- None of the pieces of writing were created at school or during school time.
- The student has not had the option to write beyond the school day or school assignments.
- The school rubric is more of a checklist type and not aligned with state or national standards.

Table 12.1 Student Portfolio for Gifted Identification in Writing – Possible Outcomes

Writing Portfolio Contents	Standardized Data	Student Self-report / Teacher Observations / Home Observations	Next Steps
All pieces in portfolio significantly exceed expectations on the rubric by two or more grade levels.	State and nationally normed tests are at or above the gifted range for writing.	Student writes in free time. During class, student is engaged in writing and in growing as a writer. Caregivers confirm student writes and tells stories "ll the time."	Complete district/state procedure for gifted identification in writing.
The writing is consistently strong and all pieces in the portfolio exceed grade level expectations by at least 2 or more grade levels.	Standardized data is in the high average range, including on writing tasks.	Student reports only writing in certain genres or on topics they find interesting. Teacher and caregiver confirm that student chooses to write in free time, but only for their own reasons.	Complete district/state procedure for gifted identification in writing.
Pieces in the portfolio show some significant strengths, but the overall quality is uneven.	Most of the standardized data is in the average range with a few spikes into high average.	Student participates in writing during class and occasionally writes at home. Student has sporadic interest in writing.	Do not pursue formal gifted identification in writing at this time. Continue providing extension and growth opportunities in writing.
Academic writing is strong and just above grade level on the rubric.	Standardized data is in the high average range.	Student does not choose writing as an activity at school or at home.	Do not pursue formal gifted identification in writing at this time. Continue providing extension and growth opportunities, especially in academic writing. Explore options for differentiation in terms of grouping or LA class placement for the student. Provide extensions and growth opportunities in writing.
Portfolio is incomplete OR only contains "canned" writing pieces that have been structured by the teacher for a very specific prompt or purpose.	Standardized data is in the average or high average range.	Student has asked to try other types of writing and requested additional time to write but isn't sure what or how. Teacher and caregiver have not observed many writing choices or behaviors.	

When collecting observations for possible gifted identification in writing, look for:

- Students who frequently choose writing during choice time.
- Students who write/draw to share with their friends, usually ongoing stories.
- Students who sneak writing when they're supposed to be doing something else.
- Students who turn every written assignment, including problem of the week in math, into a story.
- Students who write well and comfortably for any type of assignment – OR – students who write brilliantly, but only for one type of writing.

When conferring with students about a possible gifted identification in writing, ask:

- How has your writing changed over time?
- What do you like best about writing?
- What do you like least about writing?
- What are you working on right now? (This question is about writing craft skills like snappy dialog, immersive setting, writing believable characters, adding subplots, etc.)
- Do you see yourself continuing to write in high school, in college, as a possible career?

Indicators the student might need to be considered for formal gifted identification in writing are:

- The student loves to write and talk about writing.
- The student loves to read.
- The student tells great stories and has a fantastic imagination.
- The student reflects on their writing and has clear ideas about how they want to grow and improve in writing.
- The student has aspirations to publish writing someday.

Indicators the students might not need to be identified as a gifted writer at this time are:

- The student likes writing but does not love it or choose it during free time.

- The student only writes for school assignments.

- The student is interested in doing well on a rubric and getting good grades but doesn't have goals to grow in their writing craft skills.

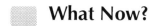 What Now?

Next Steps after Formal Gifted Identification in Writing

After an initial determination has been made and the student has a formal designation as gifted with a strength in writing, consider what differentiated instruction and programming changes might need to happen in order for the student to continuing growing as a writer. Because general education instruction for writing has such significant variance across classrooms, schools, districts, and states, the gifted specialist has a responsibility to advocate for gifted writers as well as collaborate with classroom teachers throughout the remaining years in the child's K-12 education.

Differentiation options:

- Use the extension and enrichment options for gifted writers located at the end of the most chapters in this book for daily and weekly challenges.

- Create a writing plan for the remainder of the year, mapping out required performance assessments for writing and discussing what types of writing work the student wishes to pursue outside those requirements. Use this plan to differentiate writing content, process, and product for writing assignments.

- Provide books about writing craft and mentor texts that support the student's writing development. The titles listed in Table 12.2, at the end of this section, will get you started.
- Develop and practice advocacy strategies with the student so they can ask for writing assignments to be differentiated as needed.
- Connect the student with mentor teachers and mentor writers from the community, if possible. Search "writing groups" and also search your state's name + writing project, e.g. Colorado Writing Project. Many medium and large communities offer free writing programs for tweens and teens through the local libraries as well.

Programming options:

- Confirm the student is in the advanced level/honors of Language Arts or English. In elementary school, place the student in a cluster group or cluster classroom with similarly strong and motivated readers and writers. *Put them with a teacher who is both flexible and *likes gifted kids.*
- Connect with gifted education and writing colleagues in the region, feeder, or district for help selecting the best vertical sequence of writing classes and writing instructors.
- Provide information about college- and graduate-level programs for writers.
- Provide information about multiple pathways for careers in writing.

Differentiation and programming pitfalls:

- Determining the student is "going to write a novel" and leave them alone to do that in isolation without appropriate instruction or progress monitoring.
- Forcing the student to write the things they don't like or don't care about "for growth."
- Failing to provide choices in writing throughout the year.
- Compelling the gifted writer to help reluctant/struggling writers during writing time.

Closing Thoughts About Gifted Identification in Writing

A key purpose of this book is to provide the means, motivation, and opportunity to write for every writer in your classroom. Without those three things, it is less likely a gifted student will demonstrate giftedness in writing. But **with** those three things, any writer, including those who have struggled and/or who were reluctant to write, might develop gifted behaviors and produce gifted outcomes in writing.

Am I encouraging you to push every student toward being identified as gifted in writing? Definitely not. It's just that without a writing community, writing routines, interesting meaningful writing activities, and pure, uninterrupted time to write, we can't say for sure who might be gifted in writing.

The first time through these ideas might feel challenging and messy. That's a normal writing feeling and a normal teaching feeling too. But as you hone your craft and revise, based on your own skills and the skills of this year's class, all the writing will become more habitual, more of "this is how we do this." Don't you love it when student writing is fun to read? When everyone cheers for Free Write Friday because it's the best day to settle down with a notebook or laptop and get lost in the words?

As much as I love to see a story idea unfold, I also love to see student potential grow and bloom. Writing, like teaching, is a combination of art and hard work. By choosing to work your way through this book and adding options and strategies for high potential, advanced and gifted students to your writing classroom, you've chosen a scenic byway in literacy instruction.

Thank you, I hope you enjoyed the journey.

Table 12.2 Writing Craft Books

Writing Craft Books	Type of Book	Title	Author
*Fiction – humor	Early Reader	*Mr. Putter and Tabby Write the Book*	Cynthia Ryland
*From NaNoWriMo	Middle Grade	*Brave the Page: A Young Writer's Guide to Telling Epic Stories*	Rebecca Stern & Grant Faulkner
	Middle Grade	*Writing Magic:Creating Stories that Fly*	Gail Carson Levine
	Young Adult	*Seize the Story: A Handbook for Teens Who Like to Write*	Victoria Hanley
*Appropriate for ages 13+	Adult	*The First 50 Pages*	Jeff Gerke
*Appropriate for ages 13+	Adult	*Plot versus Character*	Jeff Gerke
*Appropriate for ages 13+	Adult	*Story Genius*	Lisa Cron
*Many appropriate examples but a few from adult content books like *Mystic River*.	Adult	*Writing the Breakout Novel Workbook*	Donald Maass
Same as above	Adult	*The Emotional Craft of Fiction*	Donald Maass

Printed in the United States
by Baker & Taylor Publisher Services